VENICE IN CONTEXT

VENICE IN CONTEXT
The Independent Traveler's Guide to Venice

By

Robert S. Wayne

**INDEPENDENT
INTERNATIONAL
TRAVEL, LLC**

The first offering in the *Europe In Context* Series

www.europeincontext.com

Author Robert S. Wayne

Published by Independent International Travel, LLC © 2003

Disclaimer

The author and publisher have made their best efforts to confirm the most current data prior to publication. Prices, opening and closing times, and services are subject to change at any time. Readers should confirm prices, facilities, availabilities, services, and times when they arrive at their destination. If you find anything has changed or you want to share your travel experiences, please contact us by E-mail at: **europeincontext@mindspring.com**

Visit our Web site **www.europeincontext.com**
Or, you can send mail to:

Independent International Travel, LLC
201 Swanton Way
Decatur, Georgia 30030-3271

ISBN 0-9720228-7-2

Publisher's Cataloging-in Publication Data
(Provided by Quality Books)

Wayne, Robert S.
    Venice In Context : The Independent Traveler's Guide to Venice/
    by Robert S. Wayne.- -1st ed.
    p. cm. —(Europe, In Context)
    Includes bibliographical references and index.
    ISBN 0-9720228-7-2

    1. Venice (Italy)— Guidebooks. I. Title
    DG672.W39 2003   914.5'310493
                    QBI02-200486
    Library of Congress Catalogue Card Number: 2002108789

Front Cover: © Timothy McCarthy/Art Resource, NY
Proofreading by Bright Directions, Lawrenceville, Georgia, Rebecca Landers
CD Recording made at Allgood Studios, Atlanta, Georgia
Cover design, maps and diagrams by Renny Hart
Art pages 40, 43, 50, 73, 76, 77 Scala/Art Resource, New York
Interior photographs by Robert S. Wayne, Photograph of Joel Godard by Barney Brady
Manufactured and recorded in the United States of America
Printed and bound in Italy by L.E.G.O.

FOREWORD

I have spent many years independently exploring the treasures of Europe. I have always preferred wandering about on my own, taking time to absorb the wonderful experience of overseas travel. I have never liked being herded, rushed, or told I have to wait until the 2 o'clock tour to begin my exploration of a new city. Before embarking on a trip to a new destination, I have spent countless hours watching travel videos and reading different travel guides, art and history books, and biographies. I have often found my fellow travelers simply did not have the time to read up on what they were going to see. I have seen them spending much of their time with their heads buried in their guidebook, rather than looking up enjoying what they had come so far to see. My heart has gone out to every fellow traveler who has had to strain to hear and understand the tour guide's canned spiel, or who has had to struggle to keep up with the little lady holding aloft her umbrella or flag as she marched her bewildered tour group through the crowds.

I have taken innumerable individual tours offered by museums and city travel agencies, where I have had both wonderful and mediocre tour guides. It's simply a matter of chance.

I *knew* there had to be a better way. *Venice In Context* is the first book in my series *Europe In Context,* which offers an entirely new concept in travel guidebooks. It uses Audio CD technology to provide narrated city tours with easy-to-follow maps, backed up with detailed written information about what to see and how to get there on your own. It is designed for independent travelers who appreciate learning about a city's art and history and who want to make the most of their vacation time. This guide is the product of many hours of thought and research, coupled with long days prowling the streets and alleys of Venice. I hope you enjoy the independence it offers.

View of front of St. Mark's Basilica.

Once did She hold the gorgeous east in fee;
And was the safeguard of the west; the worth
Of Venice did not fall below her birth,
Venice, the eldest child of Liberty.
She was a maiden City, bright and free;
No guile seduced, no force could violate;
And when she took herself a Mate,
She must espouse the everlasting Sea.
And, what if she had seen those glories fade,
Those titles vanish, and that strength decay;
Yet shall some tribute of regret be paid
When her long life hath reached its final day;
Men are we, and must grieve when even the Shade
Of that which once was great is passed away

William Wordsworth
"On the Extinction of the Venetian Republic" 1807

CONTENTS

How To Use Your Audio CD Guide

Venice is filled with churches and palaces overflowing with outstanding works of art. The city also has numerous places of historical interest. Although you could spend weeks exploring this fascinating city and getting to know its people, most visitors have only a brief amount of time to experience its wonders. This guide has been designed primarily for independent travelers who prefer to enjoy a city on their own terms while making the most of their precious time. There is no need to suffer through a crowded group tour or to wait until a regularly scheduled tour begins. You no longer have to strain to hear or understand the tour guide. You no longer have to feel rushed to keep up with the tour group. Using your own personal Audio CD player and this guide, you will have the freedom to pursue your own particular interests and to explore the city at your own pace and on your own schedule.

The twelve narrated tours explore Venice in the context of its art and history. The CD narration brings the city to life with interesting anecdotes, focusing on the lives of Venice's artists, musicians, and historical figures.

Section 1, "Description of the Tours," gives a brief, written overview of the highlights of what you will see on the twelve narrated tours offered on the two CDs included with your guide. The written guide has maps of the areas explored on each tour; detailed diagrams of the three main churches visited; and many photographs of the places and works discussed on the tours. The twelve tours are arranged in a natural, geographical sequence. You may explore Venice in the order of the tours presented, or you may skip to a track that deals with a site of particular interest to you. The sites selected for these twelve tours, as well as the specific works of art discussed, were carefully chosen to illustrate Venice's long history and its rich artistic tradition.

Presenting these tours in an Audio CD format allows you to pause in mid-play during the tour narration to linger and admire a particular piece of art that intrigues you; to examine something nearby that catches your attention; or to take a break in a neighborhood café and enjoy a coffee or try some local *gelato* (Italian ice cream).

Venice's *Campanile* viewed from the balcony of St. Mark's Basilica.

Audio CD players permit you to pause or stop the play in mid-track. When you turn the CD player back on and push the play button, the track resumes playing at the point where you stopped. For the best results, use a newer sports model CD player with anti-skip protection to prevent your movements from jarring the CD play while you walk. If you use a "T-jack" and a second set of earphones, a couple traveling together can share one CD player and enjoy the narration at the same time. T-jacks are readily available at your local electronics or audio store. The twelve narrated tours can be found on the two CDs included with this guide. Each narrated tour is on a separate track just like the track of a song on a music CD. For your convenience, the number of the Tour corresponds to the Track number on each CD. Tours 1 through 5 will be found on Tracks 1 though 5 of CD One. Tours 6 through 12 will be found on Tracks 6 through 12 of CD Two. At the beginning of CD Two, there are five tracks with about four seconds of silence on each track, so that the first narrated Track containing Tour 6 begins on Track 6 of CD Two.

Directions for finding the physical starting point for each of the tours are given by the narrator at the beginning of each CD track. As much as possible, the directions avoid long, winding treks through crowded and confusing alleyways. The beginning point for each of the twelve tours is also marked with the corresponding tour number on the useful maps of the areas visited on the tours. The circled numbers on the maps indicate the starting point of each of the tours.

While you are enjoying your CD Audio tours, at certain points during the narration on each track, we will suggest that you press the pause or stop button on your CD player to allow time for you to move to the next subject described. Pause or stop your CD player when you hear the musical cue identified in the narrated introduction on Track 1. Then push the

Cafés along the *Riva del Carbon* beside the Grand Canal.

A gondola and water taxi passing along the busy Grand Canal.

play button on your CD player and resume the guide when you reach the next point identified in the narration. At the conclusion of each track, you will hear a different musical cue indicating the end of the segment, so that you can stop the CD player until you have reached the starting point for the tour covered on the next track.

Section 2, "Historical Overview," provides a summary of Venice's colorful history that will enhance your enjoyment of the tours. It is recommended that you read the Historical Overview before you begin your Audio tours.

Section 3, "Planning Your Trip," offers suggestions for planning your trip. It provides information about the sites explored on the twelve tours and tells you about other interesting places that you may wish to visit during your stay in Venice that are not covered on the narrated tours. The written guide suggests which Vaporetto line to use and identifies the landing where you should disembark to both begin each of the tours and to get to the other sites recommended in the guide.

Section 4, "A Word About Gondolas," gives you helpful tips on where and how to arrange a gondola excursion during your visit to Venice.

Section 5, "Practical Information on Vaporetti (Venice's Waterbus System)," provides information on how you can use Venice's convenient waterbus system to tour the city on your own. This section also explains

Bridge of Sighs linking the Doge's
Palace and the New Prisons.

View across the *Piazzetta* towards the Doge's
palace in the winter's fog.

how to explore the city and the outlying islands on your own using Venice's
public transportation.

Section 6, "Arriving in Venice," includes information for visitors arriving by rail, car, or air and discusses your various options for getting to and
from the airport or train station.

Section 7, "Venice Web Sites," features a number of Internet site recommendations for up-to-date information about hotels, restaurants, shop-
ping, local weather, special exhibits, and upcoming events in Venice that
will help you plan your visit before you leave on your vacation.

Section 8, "Historical Timeline," is a detailed reference, which notes
when each of the major art works examined or buildings visited during the
narrated tours was created. The timeline helps to place the lives of artists
and historical figures discussed and the important events in Venice's history in the context of other major world events.

Section 9, "Glossary," contains a dictionary of Italian words and art
terms used in the guide and in the CD narration.

Section 10, "Attraction Admission Fees and Opening Times," contains
the latest information on museum and church admission fees and opening
and closing information. It also describes the Chorus Pass offered by the

A romantic canal view.

Well-worn statue of a lion standing guard at the *Piazzetta dei Leoncini.*

Churches of Venice Association, which provides a combined entry fee to the *Basilica Santa Maria Gloriosa dei Frari* (Basilica of St. Mary in Glory of the Brothers) and fourteen of Venice's churches less frequently visited by tourists.

Inevitably, there will be times when a site covered in this guide will be closed for lunch or for renovation, or the suggested route may be blocked by construction. Relax. This is Italy, where *la dolce vita* means you have to be flexible and ready to turn a change in plans into an unexpected opportunity for adventure. Refer to the maps in this guide to find your way around any obstruction to the next site. Don't be afraid to ask for directions. Most shopkeepers speak some English. No matter where you find yourself, there will be signs indicating *"Per Rialto"* (to the Rialto Bridge) or *"Per San Marco"* (to St. Mark's Square) showing you the way that will eventually lead you back to familiar territory.

View down the Grand Canal towards the *Chiesa di Santa Maria della Salute* (the Church of St. Mary of Health) from the *Accademia* Bridge.

"It is the finest highway to be found in the whole world, lined by the finest houses, and it passes through the whole of the city."

Phillippe de Commynes, Ambassador to Venice, writing about the Grand Canal in 1495.

SECTION 1

DESCRIPTION OF THE TWELVE TOURS

TOUR 1
(CD One Track 1)

INTRODUCTION AND TOUR OF PIAZZA SAN MARCO (ST. MARK'S SQUARE) AND EXTERIOR OF BASILICA DI SAN MARCO (ST. MARK'S BASILICA)

"Venice is like eating an entire
box of chocolate liqueurs in one go."

Truman Capote

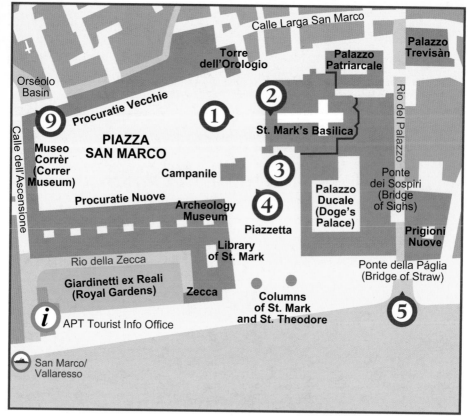

St. Mark's Square

The first tour found on Track 1 of CD One begins in *Piazza San Marco* (St. Mark's Square) in front of *Basilica di San Marco* (St. Mark's Basilica). St. Mark's Square can be reached by Vaporetto Lines 1 or 82. Get off at the *San Marco Vallaresso* landing. Walk past the *Giardinetti ex Reali* (the Royal Gardens) and the souvenir shops along the busy waterfront. Turn left at the two massive columns bearing the statues of St. Theodore and the winged lion of St. Mark and walk up the *Piazzetta di San Marco* (Little Square of St. Mark) to the front of St. Mark's Basilica where the narration for the first tour begins.

Explore the wonderful mosaics and decorative elements of St. Mark's fascinating exterior while the narrator explains the rich history of the church. Hear how the body of St. Mark the Evangelist was stolen by the

Venetians from Alexandria, Egypt, and brought to Venice. See the ancient mosaics over the portals of the basilica depicting St Mark's body being enshrined with great fanfare, as St. Mark became Venice's patron saint. Walk over to the central portal to observe the ornate Gothic carvings on the three great arches over the entrance to the basilica. Learn the stories behind the other landmarks you will find in St. Mark's Square. See the *Torre dell' Orologio* (the Clock Tower), which has an elaborate astrological clock with statues of the Virgin and Child

Carving on the arched doorway of the Basilica.

and the Lion of St. Mark. The Clock Tower is topped by the famous pair of bronze figures known as *I Mori* (the Moors) who strike the great bell each hour with their hammers.

Look across St. Mark's Square and observe the *Ala Napoleonica* (the Napoleonic Wing), which joins the wings of *Procuratie Vecchie* and *Procuratie Nuove* (the old and new Offices of the Magistrates of Venice). It now contains the *Museo Civico Correr* (the Correr Museum) with its rich

View of St. Mark's gallery overlooking St. Mark's Square.

Detail of St. Mark's exterior showing the symbols of the four Evangelists.

Close-up of mosaic with bits of colored stone depicting the head of a saint.

Mosaic from the exterior of St. Mark's Basilica.

collection of art and historical artifacts from the old Republic through Venice's reunification with Italy. Round the corner of the basilica to see the *Piazzetta dei Leoncini* (Little Square of the Lions), which takes its name from the pair of red marble statues of lions standing guard. To the right of the *Palazzo Patriarcale* (Palace of the Patriarch), home to Venice's Bishop, you will find the tomb of Venetian patriot Daniele Manin, hero of Venice's short-lived rebellion against its Austrian occupiers. Hear the story of Venice's famous rival cafés—Café Florian and Quadri's Café.

Quadri's Café.

18

TOUR 2
(CD One Track 2)

TOUR OF INTERIOR OF
BASILICA DI SAN MARCO
(ST. MARK'S BASILICA)

"Oh for one hour of blind old Dandolo,
The octogenarian chief,
Byzantium's conquering foe!"

Lord Byron,
Childe Harold's Pilgrimage

St. Mark's beautiful two-tiered pulpit.

Detail of one of the carved alabaster columns of the baldachin over the high altar.

The second tour found on Track 2 of CD One explores the exquisite interior of St. Mark's Basilica beginning with the beautiful mosaics covering the arches and six shallow domes found just inside the main door.

Basilica di San Marco (St. Mark's Basilica)
Admission free; Open Monday - Saturday 9:30 a.m. - 5:00 p.m.

Pala d'Oro (Golden Altarpiece)
Admission charge; Open weekdays 9:45 a.m. - 4:30 p.m., weekends and holy days 2:00 p.m. - 4:30 p.m.

Tesoro di San Marco (Treasury of St. Mark)
Admission charge; Open weekdays 9:45 a.m. - 4:30 p.m., weekends and holy days 2:00 p.m. - 4:30 p.m.

Museo Marciano (Museum of St. Mark) Loggia dei Cavalli (Gallery of the Horses)
Admission charge; Open Monday - Friday 9:45 a.m. - 5:00 p.m.

Listen as the narrator describes the mosaics depicting the story of creation, the lives of Noah, Abraham, and Joseph, and other Old Testament scenes. To the right of the entrance to the interior of the basilica, you will

St. Mark's interior facing towards the high altar.

St. Mark's interior facing towards the gallery over the front entrance.

View of the great choir screen dividing the nave from the chancel of St. Mark's Basilica. Atop the screen is a massive silver and gold cross.

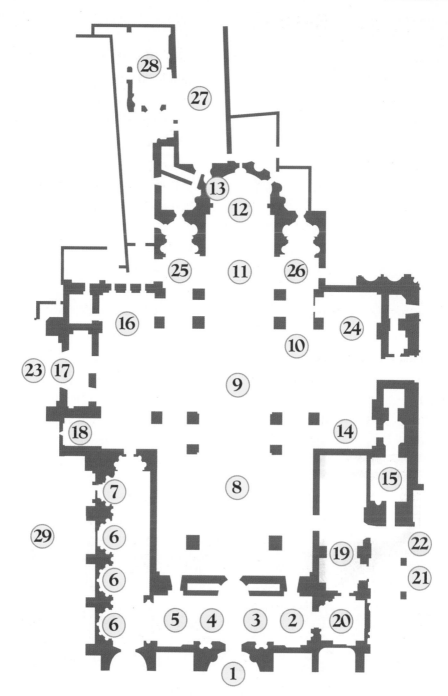

St. Mark's Basilica

St. Mark's Basilica

1. Main entrance
2. Cupola of Creation
3. Ark and the Flood
4. Death of Noah and Tower of Babel
5. Cupola of Abraham
6. Cupolas of Joseph
7. Cupola of Moses
8. Dome of the Pentecost
9. Dome of the Ascension
10. Entrance to sanctuary and Pala d'Oro (Golden Alterpiece)
11. Tomb of St. Mark the Evangelist
12. Pala d'Oro (Golden Altarpiece)
13. Sacristy door of Sansovino
14. Entrance to Treasury
15. Treasury of St. Mark's
16. Chapel with altar of the Madonna of Nicopeia
17. St. Isidore Chapel
18. Mascoli Chapel
19. Baptistery
20. Zen Chapel
21. Pillars of Acre (now thought to be from Constantinople)
22. Tetrarchs
23. Porta dei Fiori (Gate of Flowers)
24. Altar of St. Leonard
25. Chapel of St. Peter
26. Chapel of St. Clement
27. Sacristy
28. Church of St. Theodore
29. Piazzetta dei Leoncini (Little Square of the Lions)

The mosaic depicting the body of St. Mark being brought into the Basilica.

The four bronze horses of St. Mark.

see a staircase with a small sign indicating the way to the *Loggia dei Cavalli* (Gallery of the Horses). Climb the steep stairs to the second floor gallery overlooking the basilica's vast interior, glistening with mosaics and adorned with the plunder of the Fourth Crusade. Learn how the indomitable Doge Enrico Dandolo used the Fourth Crusade to enrich Venice and expand its growing commercial empire. Step outside onto the balcony and look out onto St. Mark's Square. Afterward, return inside to visit the *Museo Marciano* (Museum of St. Mark) and *Loggia dei Cavalli* (Gallery of the Horses) where you will find the four gilded bronze horses of St. Mark. Observe these magnificent works of art as the narrator recounts the legendary journeys of these bronze horses.

Go downstairs and enter the main body of St. Mark's. Listen as the narrator describes the mosaics decorating the church's main domes, the *Dome of the Pentecost* and *Dome of the Ascension*. See the great iconostasis or choir screen, with its eight columns topped by statues of the Virgin, St. Mark, and the Apostles. At the far end behind the high altar, you will find the towering mosaic *Christ Pantocrator* (Christ Almighty).

Walk past the large marble pulpit on your right where you will see the ticket desk for admission to the *Pala d'Oro* (the Golden Altarpiece). Pass through the gate and pause for a moment. Beneath the high altar, you will

Behind the *Pala d'Oro* is the altar and gilded tabernacle by Sansovino.

High altar with the tomb of St. Mark.

see the simple white tomb containing the remains of St. Mark the Evangelist. Notice the elaborately carved alabaster columns supporting the green marble canopy (called a baldachin), which covers the high altar. Hear the legend of how the body of St. Mark was miraculously revealed after being lost during the rebuilding of the basilica.

Pass around the high altar and find a place to stand to hear the description of the magnificently bejeweled Golden Altarpiece. The Altarpiece is made up of 250 enamel panels with gold and silver inlay and over 1,927 precious jewels. On the wall opposite the Golden Altarpiece you will see a small altar with a beautiful gilded bronze tabernacle door cast by Jacopo Sansovino. To its left is the large bronze door to the sacristy with reliefs depicting the dramatic scenes of *The Entombment* and *The Resurrection*. The sacristy door was also cast by Sansovino and bears portraits of the artist and his friends—Titian, Pietro Aretino, Paolo Veronese, and Andrea Palladio. Exit and return past the ticket desk. Walk to the left to visit the fabulous *Tesoro di San Marco* (the Treasury of St. Mark). It contains exquisitely jeweled chalices, cups, liturgical objects, and relics that were taken from Constantinople. The small admission fee to the Treasury includes an audio commentary on the items on display. Ask at the desk just inside the Treasury.

Before you exit St. Mark's, stop to see the sacred icon, the *Madonna of Nicopeia* (Madonna of the Bringer of Victory), which is located opposite the entrance to the Treasury. This venerated icon was brought to Venice as loot from the Fourth Crusade. Byzantine emperors once held the sacred image aloft as their armies marched into war. According to Byzantine tradition, the picture was an actual portrait of the Virgin Mary painted from life by St. Luke the Evangelist.

Unfortunately, the interior of St. Mark's is kept dimly lit for much of the day. If the basilica is not illuminated when you visit, ask one of the custodians when the interior

Bronze sacristy door sculpted and cast by Jacopo Sansovino.

lights are scheduled to be illuminated that day. If you are able to return for a second visit when the ceiling lights are on, you will be rewarded with a spectacular sight. You will understand why St. Mark's, with its shimmering interior, was known as the *Basilica d'Oro* (the Cathedral of Gold).

TOUR 3
(CD One Track 3)

TOUR OF EXTERIOR OF PALAZZO DUCALE (DOGE'S PALACE) AND THE PORTA DELLA CARTA (THE GATE OF PAPER)

"Here treachery has no place, here reigns neither the
cruelty of harlots nor the insolence of the effeminate,
O universal homeland!
Custodian of the liberties of man!
Refuge of exiles!"

Poet Pietro Aretino writing to
his patron Doge Andrea Gritti

Central window of the Doge's Palace.

The third tour found on Track 3 of CD One begins outside St. Mark's Basilica, at the corner nearest the waterfront and the *Palazzo Ducale* (the Doge's Palace). Go past the two elaborately carved white marble columns found on the south side of the basilica, the so-called *Pillars of Acre*. To the right of these white columns, you will see the statues of four small figures huddling together and clutching their swords known as the *Tetrarchs* (the four rulers). The statues are carved in red porphyry, an Egyptian stone.

Explore the beautiful Gothic exterior of the Doge's Palace and its elaborate gateway, the *Porta della Carta* (the Gate of Paper) carved by Bartolomeo Bon, whose name is carved above the doorframe. The magnificent gateway was once covered in gold leaf and connects the basilica to the Doge's Palace. Listen as the narrator describes the magnificent carved gateway with the statue of Doge Foscari kneeling before the winged lion, symbolizing the Doge's obedience to the state. At the top is the figure of Justice seated on two lions with her drawn sword in one hand and her scales of justice in the other. To the right of the entrance to the Doge's Palace and the law courts are figures depicting the *Judgment of Solomon*. Above that is the lovely figure of the *Archangel Gabriel*. Both carvings are attributed to Bartolomeo Bon. On the opposite corner nearest the waterfront is a delicate carving of the figures of *Adam and Eve*, attributed to Filippo Calendario. In the center of the Doge's Palace looking onto the *Piazetta* is the balconied window. On either side you can see the statues of various saints and on the very top is Alessandro Vittoria's statue of *Justice*.

Learn about the system of checks and balances in the government of *La Serenissima Republica di Venezia* (the Most Serene Republic of Venice) led by its Doge and the *Maggior Consiglio* (the Great Council). Though called a Republic, Venice was governed by the patrician families listed in the *Libro d'Oro* (the Golden Book). Hear about the role of the much-feared Council of Ten with its network of spies and of accusations slipped into the *Boca di Leoni* (mouth of the lions). Learn how the last Doge meekly surrendered in the face of the threat of invasion by French forces and of the terrible plunder of Venice's art treasures and wealth when Napoleon toppled the once mighty Republic of Venice.

The Archangel Gabriel.

Later on, if you have more time, you can return to visit the interior. The Doge's Palace and the courtyard are now only accessible by a combination admission ticket that also includes entry to the Correr Museum, the adjacent Archeological Musem and the Monuments Hall in the Library of St. Mark for one price as described on pages 89 and 141 through 142.

Venice Personified as Justice,
attributed to Filippo Calendario.

The Judgment of Solomon.

TOUR 4
(CD One Track 4)

TOUR OF CAMPANILE DI SAN MARCO (BELL TOWER OF ST. MARK), BIBLIOTECA MARCIANA (LIBRARY OF ST. MARK), ZECCA (VENICE'S MINT), AND THE GIARDINETTI EX REALI (THE ROYAL GARDENS)

"Venice is not only a city of fantasy and freedom.
It is also a city of joy and pleasure."

Peggy Guggenheim

Campanile of St. Mark and water-front entrance to the *Piazzetta*.

The fourth tour found on Track 4 of CD One begins across from the *Porta della Carta* (the Gate of Paper), facing the imposing *Campanile di San Marco* (the Bell Tower of St. Mark). The Bell Tower as seen today was designed by Bartolomeo Bon.

Listen to the history of the Bell Tower as you view the *Logetta's* beautiful bronze statues of Minerva, Apollo, Mercury, and Peace, and admire the marble reliefs on the upper façade sculpted by artist and architect Jacopo Sansovino. Hear how the Bell Tower suddenly collapsed into a heap of rubble on the 14th of July, 1902, and was faithfully rebuilt.

Campanile (Bell Tower)
Admission charge; Open daily 9:00 a.m. – 7:00 p.m.

Take a seat on the benches around the base of the *Loggetta* and learn about the devastation caused by the great flood that ravaged Venice in November of 1966. See the plaque marking the flood's high water mark and hear of the long-delayed plans to save Venice from the recurring threat of high water today.

Walk down the *Piazzetta di San Marco* (the Little Square of St. Mark), which is flanked by the Venetian Gothic exterior of the Doge's Palace on your left and the Renaissance facade of the *Biblioteca Marciana* (the Library of St. Mark), designed by Jacopo Sansovino, on

St. Mark's Square seen flooded by winter's high water.

31

your right. Learn why Sansovino was cast into prison by Venetian authorities after a very cold December frost.

Statue of the winged lion of St. Mark.

Continue on towards the waterfront while the narrator discusses the legends about the two great granite columns, which support statues of the two patron saints of Venice. Atop the column closest to the Library of St. Mark is the figure of St. Theodore, the city's first patron saint. St. Theodore stands in triumph above a crocodile-like dragon. The other column bears the winged lion, the traditional symbol of St. Mark. The two figures are affectionately nicknamed "Marco and Todaro" by the Venetians. Learn why superstitious Venetians still consider it bad luck to pass between these columns.

Then turn to your right and stroll along the *Molo*, the busy waterfront. Go past the *Zecca* (Venice's Mint), which was also designed by Jacopo Sansovino. Take a break in the shady and quiet *Giardinetti ex Reali* (the Royal Gardens) created by Napoleon. The public restrooms are further down on the right just past the entrance to the gardens. If you keep on walking and go past the white Venice Pavilion, which houses the main tourist information office, you will come to the world-famous Harry's Bar—birthplace of the Bellini cocktail and favorite haunt of author Ernest Hemmingway.

The quiet *Giardinetti ex Reali* (the Royal Gardens).

Piazzetta (the Little Square) with the Doge's Palace and Library of St. Mark.

TOUR 5
(CD One Track 5)

TOUR OF PONTE DEI SOSPIRI (THE BRIDGE OF SIGHS), A WALK DOWN THE RIVA DEGLI SCHIAVONI (VENICE'S WATERFRONT PROMENADE), CHIESA DI SAN ZACCARIA (THE CHURCH OF ST. ZACHARIAS), AND CHIESA DI SANTA MARIA DELLA VISITAZIONE (THE CHURCH OF THE PIETA)

"I stood in Venice on the Bridge of Sighs,
A palace and a prison on each hand."

Lord Byron,
Childe Harold's Pilgrimage

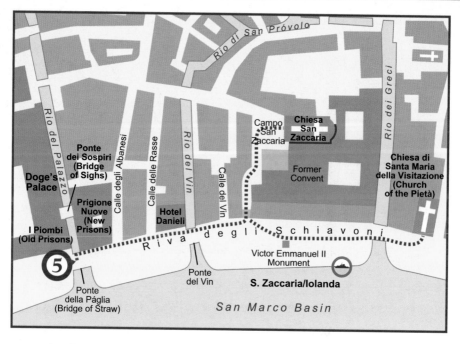

The fifth tour found on Track 5 of CD One begins at the *Ponte della Paglia* (the Bridge of Straw), where you will see the unforgettable view of the romantic *Ponte dei Sospiri* (the Bridge of Sighs). Hear how the little white bridge, built by Antonio Contino in 1614, was made famous in the 19th cen-

Calendario's *The Drunkenness of Noah.*

tury by Lord Byron. Look up to your left at the corner of the Doge's Palace, where you will find Filippo Calendario's insightful carving, *The Drunkenness of Noah*. Learn the terrible consequences of Calendario's ill-fated support of Doge Marin Falier's attempt to seize absolute power from the Great Council. Observe the *Prigioni Nuove* and *Piombe* (the New and Old Prisons) on either side of the lovely canal. Learn about the colorful life of the infamous Venetian womanizer Giovanni Giacomo Casanova, who was imprisoned here. Hear the tale of his daring escape from Venice's Inquisition and his unlikely end as a court librarian.

The Church of St. Zacharias.

Gothic arched entrance to Hotel Danieli.

Walk down the busy waterfront and see the elegant *Hotel Danieli*, a former 14th century palazzo. Then cross over the *Ponte del Vin* (the Bridge of Wine). After passing the *Calle del Vin* (Alley of Wine), take the next left under the archway marked *"sorto portico San Zaccaria,"* which will lead you to the peaceful *Campo San Zaccaria* (Square of St. Zacharias), where you will find the beautiful *Chiesa di San Zaccaria* (the Church of St. Zacharias).

Church of St. Zacharias

Admission to church free, admission charge to Chapel of St. Tarasius; Open daily 10:00 a.m. – 12:00 a.m., 4:00 p.m. – 6:00 p.m.

Learn the history behind this Benedictine Convent, which grew so rich and powerful that it acquired the entire bodies of nine saints, including the body of St. Zacharias, the father of John the Baptist, to whom they dedicated this church.

Enter the church to admire Giovanni Bellini's serene masterpiece, *Madonna and Child with Saints.* On the opposite wall, you will find the silver-clad tomb of St. Zacharias. To the left of the tomb, you will find the ticket desk for entry into the Chapel of St. Tarasius. Go through the Chapel of St. Athanasius, where you will see the *Birth of St. John the Baptist*, an early painting by Tintoretto. See the elaborate chairs used by the Doge during his annual pilgrimage to the convent. Pass through the door on your left to enter the Chapel of St. Tarasius as the narrator describes its early Renaissance ceiling frescos painted by the Florentine Andrea del Castagno and the elaborate Gothic altarpieces by Antonio Vivarini and Giovanni d'Alemagna. Go down the steps leading underneath the Chapel of St. Tarasius and peer into the church's dark, watery 9th century crypt, where the remains of eight early Doges lie buried.

Bellini's *Madonna and Child with Saints.*

Return to the waterfront and turn left. Proceed along Venice's busy promenade, the *Riva degli Schiavoni*, to the equestrian statue of Victor Emmanuel II, first King of a United Italy. Find out about the *Risorgimento* movement and Italy's long and turbulent struggle for unification. Continue on, crossing the bridge over the *Rio Dei Greci* (River of the Greeks), until you reach the beautiful *Chiesa di Santa Maria della Visitazione,* (the Church of the Pieta), designed by Giorgio Massari. It was the former

church of a 14th century orphanage for girls where they received special musical training. It is now a frequent site of evening concerts. Hear the story of the life of Venetian native Antonio Vivaldi, the well-known composer and concert-master of the Church of the Pieta, and learn of his sad end.

On the base of the statue of Victor Emmanuel II, beneath the Lion's paw, you can find the final tally of the votes cast by the Venetians who voted to join the Kingdom of Italy in 1866.

TOUR 6
(CD Two Track 6)

TOUR OF SCUOLA DI SAN GIORGIO
DEGLIA SCHIAVONI
(SCHOOL OF ST. GEORGE OF THE DALMATIANS)

"In the winter, Venice is like an abandoned theater.
The play is finished, but the echoes remain."

Robert Burton

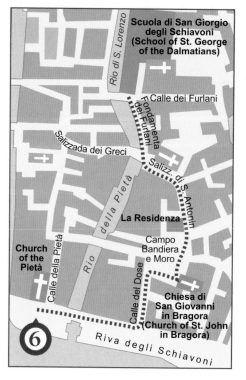

The sixth tour found on Track 6 of CD Two begins in front of the Church of the Pieta, which can be reached by Vaporetto Lines 1, 82, or 52. Get off at the *San Marco* or *San Zaccaria* Vaporetto landing. Walk past the Church of the Pieta along the waterfront. Pass *Calle della Pietà* and cross over the next bridge. Then turn left onto *Calle del Dose*, which will shortly lead you to the quiet *Campo Bandiera e Moro* (Square of Bandiera and Moro), dedicated to two early Venetian patriots and martyrs of the *Risorgimento* movement.

In the square, you will find the simple façade of *Chiesa di San Giovanni in Bragora* (the Church of St. John in Bragora). If the church is open you may wish to pause your CD player and step inside. The interior of this simple church contains many astonishingly beautiful works. You will find Bartolomeo Vivarini's *Madonna and Child with Saints* located in the

Salizzada del Sant' Antonin.

Facade of the Church of St. John in Bragora.

Chapel to the left as you enter, and Cima da Conegliano's magnificent *Baptism of Christ* is over the high altar.

Cross the square and walk to the right around the corner of *La Residenza*, the Gothic palace of a former Doge. Bear left onto the picturesque *Salizzada del Sant' Antonin*. At the end of the *Salizzada*, you will come to a canal. Turn right up the *Fondamenta Dei Furlani*. Walk the short distance along the canal to the front of the *Scuola di San Giorgio degli Schiavoni* (the School of St. George of the Dalmatians), where the narration continues.

View of façade of the School of St. George of the Dalmatians.

School of St. George

Admission charge; Open Tuesday - Saturday 10:00 a.m. - 12:00 p.m., 3:30 p.m. - 6:30 p.m., Sunday 10:00 a.m. - 12:30 p.m.

The School of St. George of the Dalmatians served the humble, working-class community from the east coast of former Yugoslavia. The people of Dalmatia were called the *Schiavoni* (big slaves) by the Venetians. Built for the lay brotherhood of the Dalmatian community living in Venice, this is one of the best-preserved of such schools in Venice. The façade was built in 1551 by Giovanni de Zan. Over the entrance is a fine relief of St. George on horseback slaying the dragon, and a relief of the *Madonna and Child*. Step inside this exquisite Renaissance jewel and pay the small admission at the desk just to your left as you enter. Take a seat and listen as the narrator describes Vittore Carpaccio's astonishing series of paintings depicting scenes from the lives of Saints George, Jerome, and Tryphon. Find out about the special role played in Venetian life by the religious associations of laypersons known as the *scuole*. Walk up the stairs located to the left of the high altar to see the 15th century meeting room, where members of the lay brotherhood gathered for religious services and to discuss the concerns of their community.

The walls of the small the School of St. George of the Dalmatians are lined with works by Vittore Carpaccio.

Vittore Carpaccio's famous *Vision of St. Augustine in His Study*.

T O U R 7
(CD Two Track 7)

TOUR OF CHIESA DI SAN GIORGIO MAGGIORE (THE CHURCH OF ST. GEORGE MAJOR)

"Italia! O Italia!
thou who hast
The fatal gift of beauty."

Lord Byron,
Childe Harold's Pilgrimage

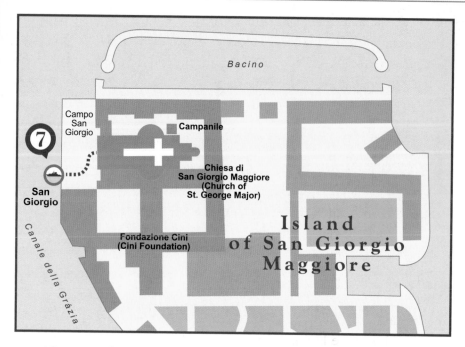

The seventh tour found on Track 7 of CD Two explores the *Chiesa di San Giorgio Maggiore* (the Church of St. George Major), which is located on the small island across the San Marco Basin from the Doge's Palace. Begin your tour standing in front of the dramatic *Chiesa di San Giorgio Maggiore* (the Church of St. George Major). You can reach the Church of St. George Major on Vaporetto Line 82, departing from the *San Zaccaria* Vaporetto landing on the *Riva degli Schiavoni* near the equestrian statue of Victor Emmanuel II. When you cross the San Marco Basin, get off at the *San Giorgio* Vaporetto landing.

Church of St. George Major and Bell Tower
Admission to church is free, Bell Tower admission charge;
Open daily 9:30 a.m. - 12:30 p.m., 2:30 p.m. - 6:00 p.m.

Observe the beautiful exterior of the Church of St. George Major and listen as the narrator tells the story of the Benedictine monks who established their monastery here in the 10th century on the island once called the "island of the cypresses." When the relics of St. Stephen were brought here from Constantinople in 1009, the monastery grew wealthy from pilgrims and became a center of learning. Learn about the life of the church's architect, Andrea di Pietro della Gondoa, nicknamed "Palladio" for Pallas Athena, the Greek Goddess of Wisdom. Influenced by the classical architecture of ancient Rome, the "Palladian style," as it came to be known, became very popular in 18th century England and later in America.

Go inside the church to the high altar, where you will see the fine bronze sculpture group by Girolamo Campagna, with a statue of Christ atop a gleaming golden orb supported by the Evangelists and Angels. Hear about the life of Jacopo Robusti, nicknamed "Tintoretto" (the little dyer), the master of the Venetian High Renaissance. On the walls on either side of the high altar, you can admire the two final paintings of his long and productive life, *The Last Supper* and *The Shower of Manna*.

Tintoretto's distinctive style can be seen in *The Last Supper*. It is a whirlwind of movement by the Apostles and their servants. Angels appear to emerge from the billowing smoke of the lamp and from the shadows in the room. This is the last of eight versions of *The Last Supper* painted by Tintoretto in his long career in Venice. On your left, you will see Tintoretto's *The Shower of Manna*. These two works were painted in the

Tintoretto's mystical *The Last Supper* found to the right of the high altar of the Church of St. George Major.

View of the Church of St. George Major as seen across the San Marco Basin.

last two years of Tintoretto's life, before he died in the plague of 1594 at the age of 76.

Walk behind the main altar. You will find intricately carved 16th century choir stalls. Look closely and you can see they are embellished with carvings of winged lions and are topped by whimsical cherubs riding seahorses. Learn about the history of the church and its monastery. Pope Pius VII was elected here in 1800 in defiance of Napoleon, when the conclave took shelter in Venice from French troops threatening Rome. Find out about Napoleon's terrible revenge. Wander the interior of the church and see the other fine works of art by Jacopo da Bassano, Sebastiano Ricci, and Vittore Carpaccio.

Walk through the doors located to the left of the choir. For a small fee, you can take the lift to the top of the church's Bell Tower, which offers a breathtaking view of Venice, including the Doge's Palace, the Bell Tower of St. Mark, and St. Mark's Basilica across the Basin. From the Bell Tower, you can look down on the old monastery and grounds adjacent to the church, which are now part of the Giorgio Cini Foundation. The Cini Foundation is dedicated to preserving Venetian culture, but the buildings of the old monastery are only open for special occassions.

TOUR 8
(CD Two Track 8)

TOUR OF BASILICA DI SANTA MARIA GLORIOSA DEI FRARI (BASILICA OF ST. MARY IN GLORY OF THE BROTHERS)

"The surface of Venice is constantly metamorphosing
[and] painting Venice is almost like being
a restorer, peeling off the layers to find the
picture after picture underneath."

Quoted by Erica Jong
"A City of Love and Death: Venice"
NY Times, March 23, 1986

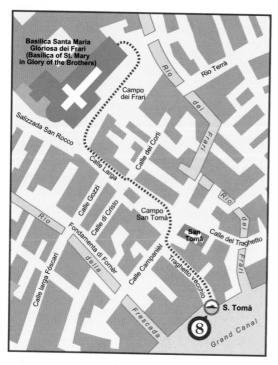

The eighth tour found on Track 8 of CD Two explores the *Basilica Santa Maria Gloriosa dei Frari* (Basilica of St. Mary in Glory of the Brothers). The church is known in Venice simply as the *Frari,* which is Italian for "brothers." The beautiful Gothic church is located in the *San Polo* district and can be reached by Vaporetto Lines 1 or 82. Get off at the *San Toma* Vaporetto landing, exiting onto *Calle del Traghetto Vecchio.* At the end of the *Calle,* turn right onto *Calle del Campaniel.* Go to *Campo San Toma* (St. Thomas Square). Turn left, crossing the square. Pass around to the right of the building at the far end. Turn left at the rear corner of the church onto *Calle Dei Corli,* before taking an immediate right up *Calle Largo.* Directly ahead will be the side of the church of the Frari. At the end of *Calle Largo,* turn right and walk along the side of the church to the front entrance, where the narrative begins.

Basilica of St. Mary in Glory of the Brothers

Admission charge; Open weekdays 9:00 a.m. - 6:00 p.m., Sundays and holy days 1:00 p.m. - 6:00 p.m.

Basilica of St. Mary in Glory of the Brothers.

View inside the church towards Titian's *Assumption of the Virgin* as seen through the ornate choir screen.

View towards Titian's *Ca' Pesaro altarpiece,* and the tombs of Doge Giovanni Pesaro and sculptor Antonio Canova.

A statue of the *Risen Christ* by Alessandro Vittoria stands over the arched doorway of the imposing late Gothic façade. On either side of the entrance are statues of the *Virgin* and *St. Francis,* both by Bartolomeo Bon. Retrace your steps to the side entrance. After paying the admission, turn to your right and walk to the center of the church to get a sense of the immense interior. Construction was begun on this church in 1330 by the Order of Franciscan Brothers. The church became richly endowed with astonishing works of art and with the imposing tombs of many notable Venetians, including artists Titian and Antonio Canova, and several illustrious Doges, including Doge Francesco Foscari.

Walk away from the high altar towards the back of the church. On the left you will see the tall, white, monumental tomb of Tiziano Vecellio, known as "Titian." Hear the life story of this genius who dominated the Venetian High Renaissance and enjoyed the first truly international artistic career. Discover the subtle clue to the ulterior motives of the Austrian Hapsburg rulers, who erected this elaborate tomb to honor Venice's famous son.

Across from Titian's tomb you will find the striking, pyramid-shaped, neoclassical monument containing the heart of the 19th century sculptor

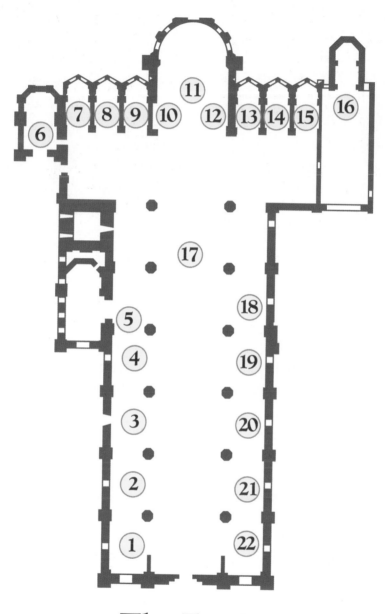

The Frari

BASIILCA OF ST. MARY IN GLORY OF THE BROTHERS (THE FRARI)

1. Chapel of the Crucifixion, designed by Baldassare Longhena, executed by Justin Le Court
2. Tomb of Antonio Canova, designed by Canova (originally intended as a memorial to Titian)
3. Monument to Doge Giovanni Pesaro, designed by Baldassare Longhena, and statues by Melchiorre Barthel and Bernardo Falcone
4. Titian's Ca' Pesaro Madonna (Virgin of the Pesaro Family)
5. Tomb of Bishop Jacopo Pesaro, by Tullio and Antonio Lombardo
6. Corner Chapel with Bartolomeo Vivarini's St. Mark Triptych and Jacopo Sansovino's St. John the Baptist
7. Chapel of the Milanese with tomb of Monteverdi; above, Alvise Vivarini and Marco Basaiti's St. Ambrose with Saints
8. Chapel of St. Michael with Giuseppe Angeli's Immaculate Conception
9. Chapel of the Franciscan Saints with Bernardino Licinio's Madonna and Child with Six Saints
10. Tomb of Doge Nicolo Tron by Antonio Rizzo
11. Titian's Assumption of the Virgin
12. Tomb of Doge Foscari, attributed to Antonio and Paolo Bregno
13. Chapel of the Florentines with Donatello's St. John the Baptist
14. Chapel of the Holy Sacrament
15. Bernardo Chapel with Bartolomeo Vivarini's polyptych, Virgin Enthroned with Child and Saints
16. Sacristy with Giovanni Bellini's Madonna and Child with Four Saints
17. Choir stalls carved by Marco Cozzi, with bronze crucifix by Andrea del Verrocchio; Choir screen by Bartolomeo Bon and Pietro Lombardo
18. Altar with Jacopo Palma, the Younger's Martyrdom of St. Catherine
19. Altar with Giuseppe Nogari's St. Joseph of Copertino, and Alessandro Vittoria statues of St. Jerome flanked by St. Peter (r) and St. Andrew (l)
20. Altar of the Presentation of Jesus at the Temple designed by Baldassare Longhena, executed by Giuseppe Salviati
21. Tomb of Titian by Luigi and Pietro Zandomeneghi
22. Altar of St. Anthony designed by Baldassare Longhena, executed by Giuseppe Sard

Titian's ground breaking *Ca' Pesaro Madonna*.

Tomb of Doge Foscari.

Tomb of sculptor Antonio Canova.

Antonio Canova. Walk to your right past the colossal Baroque monument to Doge Giovanni Pesaro, which was designed by Baldassare Longhena. Then go over to admire Titian's painting *Virgin of the Pesaro Family*, which is located on your left. Listen as the narrator describes Titian's ground-breaking painting, which commemorates the defeat of the Turks in the naval battle of *Santa Maura* in 1502.

Continue on to the front of the church passing though the elaborate marble choir screen carved by Bartolomeo Bon and Pietro Lombardo. Turn left and go to the third chapel on the left from the central altar. Pause to hear about the life of composer Claudio Monteverdi. He is buried here in a simple grave beneath the painting *St. Ambrose with Saints* by Alvise Vivarini and Marco Basaiti. Go through the door on the left to enter the Corner Chapel, where you will find a wonderful Gothic altarpiece, the *St. Mark Triptych,* by Bartolomeo Vivarini, and the baptismal font and statue of *St. John the Baptist* by Jacopo Sansovino.

Then walk over to the central chapel with the high altar to see Titian's triumphant masterpiece, *Assumption of the Virgin,* which he completed in 1518. At first, this huge painting confounded the Franciscan brothers, but it established Titian's reputation as the preeminent artist of his time. Standing 22 feet in height and 11 feet in width, this colossal painting, was the largest oil painting on canvas ever painted up to that time.

Look to the right of the high altar and see the marble-draped Gothic tomb of Doge Francesco Foscari, Venice's longest-reigning Doge, while you hear the dark tale of how Foscari fell from power through the intrigue of his rivals – the Loredan family. Walk over to the first Chapel to the right of the high altar to admire Donatello's poignant statue of *St. John the Baptist*. It is located in the Chapel of the Florentines, where the

Alessandro Vittoria's *St. Jerome.*

Florentine community living in Venice gathered to worship.

Continue walking to the right and pass through the door into the quiet sacristy. Turn left as you enter and take a seat to contemplate Giovanni Bellini's serene masterpiece, *Virgin and Child with Saints*. Hear the account of the successful Bellini family workshop, which was founded by Jacopo Bellini with his talented sons, Gentile and Giovanni. Discover the innovation mastered by Giovanni Bellini that profoundly impacted the development of Renaissance art and made him the most sought-after artist of his generation.

There is so much to see in this remarkable church. Take your time to simply wander around and explore its unsurpassed art treasures. Many of these works of art are identified in this guide. Be sure not to miss Jacopo Palma the Younger's *Martyrdom of St. Catherine* and the statue of *St. Jerome with Sts. Peter and Andrew* carved by Venetian native Alessandro Vittoria.

TOUR 9
(CD Two Track 9)

TOUR OF BACINO ORSEOLO (ORSEOLO BASIN) AND THE STORY OF THE GONDOLA

"And at night they sang in the gondolas,
and in the barche with lanterns;
the prows rose silver on silver,
taking light in the darkness."

Ezra Pound

 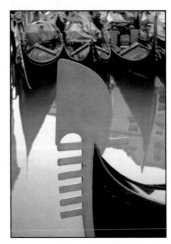

Views of gondolas moored in the Orseolo Basin.

To reach the site discussed on the ninth tour found on Track 9 of CD Two, begin in St. Mark's Square, near the *Ala Napoleonica* (the Napoleonic Wing), at the end opposite from St. Mark's Basilica (See map page 16). With St. Mark's Basilica to your back, walk past the crowds and pigeons to the far right corner of the Square, and then go through the passageway to the *Bacino Orseolo* (Orseolo Basin). It is named for the Orseolo family, whose palace once stood near this site.

Hear about the Orseolo family and Doge Pietro Orseolo II's great victory against the Adriatic pirates in the year 1000. This victory has been commemorated since that time by the elaborate symbolic ceremony of

Sposalizio del Mare (Venice's Wedding to the Sea). While you watch the gondoliers gathering in the Orseolo basin to arrange gondola excursions for visitors, learn about the history of the gondola and the symbolism of its traditional decorations.

The *Squero di San Trovaso*, one of the last surviving gondola workshops in Venice.

TOUR 10
(CD Two Track 10)

TOUR OF PONTE DI RIALTO (THE RIALTO BRIDGE), CAMPO, AND CHIESA DI SAN GIACOMO DI RIALTO (THE SQUARE AND CHURCH OF ST. JAMES)

"I will buy with you, sell with you, talk with you,
walk with you, and so following;
but I will not eat with you, drink with you,
nor pray with you. What news on the Rialto?"

William Shakespeare,
The Merchant of Venice

The tenth tour found on Track 10 of CD Two begins on the Grand Canal at the base of the steps to *Ponte di Rialto* (the Rialto Bridge). You can get there on Vaporetto Lines 1 or 82. Disembark at the *Rialto* Vaporetto landing. Turn left and walk up *Riva del Ferro* to the platform at the base of the stairs leading up to the Rialto Bridge, where the narrative begins.

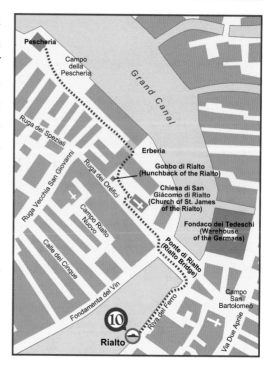

Learn about the history of the Rialto Bridge. The white stone bridge that spans the Grand Canal today was erected in 1591. A competition was held to choose the design of the bridge. You will be surprised at the famous artists whose designs were rejected. The winner was a little-known city engineer, the aptly named Antonio da Ponte (Anthony of the Bridge).

Walk to the center of the Bridge and look out over the water. Take a few moments out from your tour to survey the many types of boats that ply the busy waters of the Grand Canal and pass under the Rialto Bridge. The bridge is always crowded with tourists visiting the many shops that line the

Antonio da Ponte's beautiful Rialto Bridge spanning the Grand Canal.

The front of the Church of St. James of the Rialto.

The *Gobbo di Rialto* (the Hunchback of the Rialto).

three lanes of the bridge. When you are ready to proceed, walk down the steps on the other side of the bridge. You will see a bell tower ahead to your right. Continue on until you reach the *Campo San Giacomo di Rialto* (the Square of St. James of the Rialto). This area was the former epicenter of Venice's vast commercial empire. Today, it is still a busy marketplace. Learn about the commercial innovations that were first developed by the merchants who gathered on this spot to manage their far-flung business ventures.

You will see the *Chiesa di San Giacomo di Rialto* (the Church of St. James of the Rialto), recognizable by its unique Gothic porch and 15th century clock tower. If the church is open, pause your CD player and step inside the dark interior of the domed church. Built in the shape of a Greek cross in the Byzantine style, it is thought to be the oldest church in Venice. Over the high altar, you will find Alessandro Vittoria's statue of *St. James with Angels.*

Walk away from the church towards the other side of the busy square, where you will find the 16th century statue *Gobbo di Rialto* (the Hunchback

For over a thousand years, Venetians have gathered here at the fruit and vegetable market to shop for their family's dinner.

of the Rialto). This crouched figure supports the platform from which state proclamations were read to the assembled crowds. Pass under the arcade to your right to experience the colorful *Erberia* (the fruit and vegetable market). Continue on to the bustling and fragrant *Campo de Peschieria* (the local fish market). In the morning, this area is packed with Venetians going about their daily lives. The wonderful seafood special you may be served at dinner tonight was probably bought here that very morning. You might find this delightful area a perfect place to be brave and wander off the beaten track to explore. There are many different shops, souvenir stands, and fine restaurants nearby. When you are ready to return, just look for the signs indicating the way to the Rialto Bridge, *"Per Rialto."* If you follow these signs, they will eventually lead you back to the Rialto Bridge, where this tour began.

T O U R   1 1
(CD Two Track 11)

TOUR OF CHIESA DI SANTA MARIA DELLA SALUTE
(THE CHURCH OF ST. MARY OF HEALTH) AND THE DOGANA DI MARE (VENICE'S CUSTOMHOUSE)

"Time flows when you rest your elbows on
the ledges of Venetian windows"

Henry James

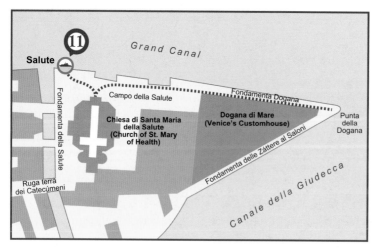

The eleventh tour found on Track 11 of CD Two begins in front of the stunning *Chiesa di Santa Maria della Salute* (the Church of St. Mary of Health), which was designed by Baldassare Longhena. The Church of St. Mary of Health can be reached by Vaporetto Line 1. Get off at the *Salute* Vaporetto landing, which is located directly in front of the church.

Learn how *Chiesa di Santa Maria della Salute* (the Church of St. Mary of Health) was built by the city of Venice to give thanks to the Madonna

Longhena's Baroque high altar with the venerated icon known as *Madonna of Health*.

Close-up of volute supporting the dome of the Church of St. Mary of Health.

Church of St. Mary of Health.   Venice's Customhouse.

for the end of the terrible plague of 1630 in which a third of her population perished.

Church of St. Mary of Health
Admission to church free, admission charge to sacristy; Open
Monday - Sunday 9:00 a.m. – 12:00 p.m., 3:00 p.m. - 5:30 p.m.

Walk up the steps and enter the church. Turn and walk clockwise around the perimeter of the church's octagonal rotunda. See the intricate patterns of the polychrome mosaic floor in the center of the great rotunda. Pause at the third chapel you come to, where you will find Titian's magnificent painting *The Pentecost.* Continue on to the central chapel, which is dominated by an ornate Baroque high altar, designed by Baldassare Longhena. The high altar is decorated with an elaborate sculptural group executed by Flemish sculptor Justin le Court, depicting *Venice's Liberation from the Plague.* Below is the miraculous icon known as the *Madonna of Health* or the *Black Madonna,* another work once believed to have been painted by St. Luke.

Walk to the left of the high altar where you will find the door leading to the church's sacristy. After paying the small admission fee, you can see several Venetian masterworks, including thirteen paintings by Titian, including his early painting of *St. Mark Enthroned*. Learn about the four saints shown in the painting, who were associated with prayers for deliverance from the plague (represented as a dark shadow falling over St. Mark's face). On the ceiling you will see Titian's *Cain and Abel, The Sacrifice of Abraham,* and *David and Goliath.*

On the long wall to your right is Tintoretto's *Marriage At Cana.* This painting was hailed by the preeminent Victorian art critic John Ruskin as one of the world's greatest art treasures. Exit the sacristy and finish your circumnavigation around the rotunda to admire the church's other fine works of art by Lucca Giordano and Pietro Liberi.

Exit the church. Turn right. Walk past the arched doors of the former warehouses until you reach the very tip of the promontory at the point where the Grand Canal empties into the San Marco Basin. Here you can enjoy a sweeping view of Venice, which stretches down to the *Giardini Pubblici* (the Public Gardens) located at the very end of the island and encompasses the *Chiesa di San Giorgio Maggiore* (the Church of St. George Major) across the water. Turn around to admire the 17th century *Dogana di Mare* (Venice's Customhouse). Built of brilliant white stone, the customhouse is topped by two crouching bronzed figures of Atlas, bearing a huge golden globe on their backs. Balanced on top of the golden sphere is the statue of Fortune.

You might want to walk to the left and pass around the tip of the promontory and stroll along the *Fondamenta della Zattere.* It takes its name from the *zattere* (the floating rafts) that once docked along the shore bringing wood from the mainland. You will enjoy lovely views to the island of the *Giudecca* and you can see Andrea Palladio's last contribution to the architecture of Venice, *Il Redentore* (Church of the Redeemer). Further down, you will come to pleasant waterside cafés. Or, you may retrace your steps to the *Salute* landing and follow the signs to visit Peggy Guggenheim's fascinating collection of modern art, housed in the 18th century *Palazzo Venier dei Leoni* (Venier Palace of the Lions).

TOUR 12
(CD Two Track 12)

TOUR OF CAMPO AND CHIESA DEI SANTI GIOVANNI E PAOLO
(SQUARE AND CHURCH OF SAINTS JOHN AND PAUL)

"When I went to Venice, I discovered that
my dream had become—incredibly
but quite simply—my address."

Marcel Proust

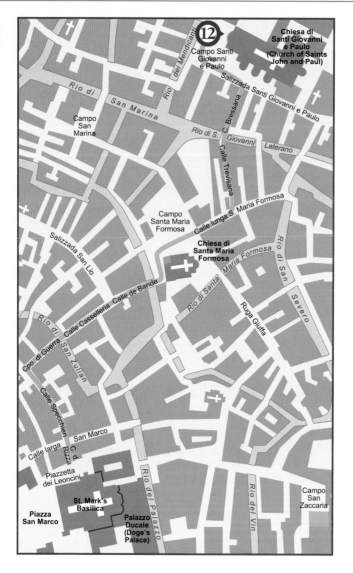

The twelfth and final tour found on Track 12 of CD Two begins in the *Campo* and *Chiesa di Santi Giovanni e Paolo* (the Square and Church of Saints John and Paul). The church is also known, in the slurred Venetian dialect, as "*San Zanipolo.*" To get there on foot, start from the *Piazzetta dei Leoncini* (Little Square of the Lions) located on the north side of St. Mark's Basilica just down from the *Torre dell' Orologio* (the Clock Tower). Turn left into *Calle della Rizza*—the last *Calle* out of *Piazzetta dei Leoncini*. It quickly becomes *Calle Specchieri*. Walk down the long *Calle Specchieri* until you reach the rough brick exterior at the back of the church of *San Zulian* on your left. It is not marked, but you will see the church's bell tower overhead as you approach. *Campo De Guerra* will be on your right. Turn right and go into *Campo De Guerra*. Proceed over the small bridge on the other end onto *Calle Casselleria*. This turns into *Calle De Bande* once you pass over the next bridge.

Chiesa Santi Giovanni e Paolo
(Church of Saints John and Paul).

You will then come to the Church of *Santa Maria Formosa*. The church was rebuilt for the wealthy Cappello family by Mauro Codussi in about 1492. If the church is open, it is worth a quick visit. The church houses the heroic *St. Barbara,* a masterpiece by Palma the Elder, and Bartolomeo Vivarini's *Madonna of Mercy.*

Pass around to the left of the church into the large *Campo Santa Maria Formosa.* Cross the square and go to *Calle Lunga Santa Maria Formosa.* Walk down *Calle Lunga* and watch for the fourth *Calle* on the left—*Calle Trevisana Cicogna.* There you will see signs indicating the way to "*San Giovanni*" and "*Colleoni*" and a faded blue and white sign pointing the way to the "*Ospedale*" (the hospital).

The wellhead, adorned with *putti* and garlands, stands beside the *Chiesa Santi Giovanni e Paolo* (Church of Saints John and Paul).

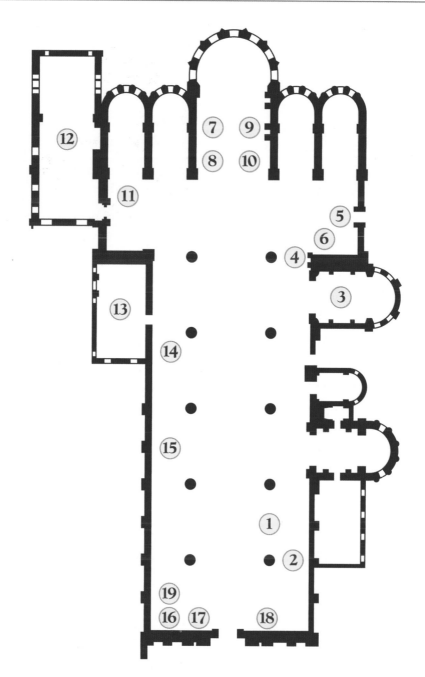

Santi Giovanni e Paulo
("San Zanipolo")

CHURCH OF STS. JOHN AND PAUL (SAN ZANIPOLO)

1. Altar, with Giovanni Bellini's St. Vincent Ferrer, a Pieta between two panels of an Annunciation (above), St. Christopher (left), and St. Anthony (right); predella with scenes from the life of St. Ferrer (below)

2. Monument to Marcantonio Bragadin

3. Chapel of St. Dominic, with Giovanni Battista Piazzetta's Glory of St. Dominic

4. Relic of St. Catherine of Siena

5. Gothic stained glass window by Gian Antonio Licinio da Lodi

6. Cima da Conegliano's Coronation of the Virgin

7. Tomb of Doge Andrea Vendramin, by Tullio and Antonio Lombardo

8. Tomb of Doge Marco Corner, with statue of the Madonna by Nino Pisano

9. Tomb of Doge Leonardo Loredan, designed by Girolamo Grapiglia, and statue by Girolamo Campagna

10. Tomb of Doge Michele Morosini from the dalle Masegne school

11. Tomb of Doge Sebastiano Venier, with statue by Antonio Dal Zotto

12. Rosary Chapel with Veronese's Annunciation, Assumption, and Adoration of the Shepherds

13. Sacristy

14. Tomb of Doge Pasquale Malipiero, by the Lombardo family

15. Tomb of Doge Tommaso Mocenigo, by Piero di Niccolo Lamberti and Giovanni di Martino

16. Tomb of Doge Giovanni Mocenigo, by Tullio Lombardo

17. Tomb of Doge Alvise Mocenigo, by the Lombardo family

18. Tomb of Doge Pietro Mocenigo, by the Lombardo family

19. Altar of Verde Scaligera, with statue of St. Jerome by Alessandro Vittoria

Andrea del Verrocchio's powerful
bronze figure of Bartolomeo Colleoni.

Turn left down *Calle Trevisana Cicogna*. At the end of the *Calle,* you will take a short right turn, then left over the bridge. Directly ahead through the passageway *Calle Bressana,* you will see the side of the towering *Chiesa dei Santi Giovanni e Paolo* (the Church of Saints John and Paul). The narration begins in the square near the equestrian statue of Bartolomeo Colleoni, by Andrea del Verrocchio. The entire walk takes about twenty-five minutes.

If you wish to avoid the winding walk, you may get to the Square and Church of Saints John and Paul by taking Vaporetto Line 52. The pleasant boat ride takes about thirty-five minutes. Board the Vaporetto at the *San Zaccaria* Vaporetto landing near the Hotel Danieli and disembark at the *Ospedale Civile* Vaporetto landing. Turn right and walk down *Fondamenta Nuove* with the water on your right. Just before the first bridge over the *Rio dei Mendicanti* (Canal of the Beggars), turn left and go down the *Fondamenta dei Mendicanti.* The square with the *Scuola di San Marco* (School of St. Mark) and the Church of Saints John and Paul will be down on your left.

Once you reach the square, walk over to the equestrian statue of the famed *condottiere* (mercenary general) Bartolomeo Colleoni, which you will see atop a high pedestal. The striking statue was designed by the Florentine Andrea del Verrocchio, but was cast by Venetian native Alessandro Leopardi four years after Verrocchio's untimely death. Leopardi's name is emblazoned on the pedestal, but you will search in vain for any mention of Verrocchio.

To the left of the entrance to the church is the wonderfully ornate façade of the *Scuola di San Marco* (the School of St. Mark) with its *trompe l'oeil* panels by Pietro Lombardo and Giovanni Buora. The upper stories were completed by Mauro Codussi. Above the door, is a particularly fine relief representing *St. Mark with the Brethren of the Scuola*. Above that is a statue of *Charity*. Both works are attributed to Bartolomeo Bon. After the Dominican monastery was closed by Napoleon, the building was used as a military hospital. Today it is home to the *Ospedale Civile* (the City Hospital).

Church of Saints John and Paul

Admission free; Open Monday - Saturday 7:30 a.m. - 12:30 p.m., 3:00 p.m. - 7:00 p.m.; Sunday 3:00 p.m. - 6:00 p.m.

Stained glass windows by Gian Antonio Licinio da Lodi.

Go inside and explore the rich holdings of the Church of Saints John and Paul, which was built by the Order of Dominican Friars. Construction was begun in the 13th century, but was not completed until well into the 15th century. It is considered the "Pantheon of Venice" and holds the tombs of twenty-seven Doges. To the right as you enter, you will come upon the altar with Giovanni Bellini's early painting of the Dominican St. Vincent Ferrer. To the right of the Bellini painting is the tomb of Marcantonio Bragadin, famous as the "Defender of Famagusta," Venice's last stronghold in Cyprus. Learn of Bragadin's horrific death at the hands of the Turks. Continue walking further down the aisle. Pause to admire a masterpiece of the 18th century, the Baroque Chapel of St. Dominic with its fabulous ceiling painting *St. Dominic in Glory,* by Giovanni Battista Piazzetta.

After you pass the altar with the small relic of St. Catherine, turn to your right, where you will see the stunning stained glass windows by Gian Antonio Licinio da Lodi. On the wall just to the right of the windows is Cima da Conegliano's painting *The Coronation of the Virgin.*

Walk to the center of the transept to observe the magnificent high altar designed by Baldassare Longhena. To the left of the high altar is the tomb of

Side view of the Church with the statue of Colleoni atop its pedestal.

Tomb of Doge Pietro Mocenigo.

Doge Andrea Vendramin, sculpted by Antonio and Tullio Lombardo. Opposite that is the tomb of Doge Leonardo Loredan, by Giovanni Grapiglia. Hear the story of how the clever Doge Loredan saved Venice from the mighty alliance of Europe's great powers known as the League of Cambrai.

Walk to the left of the high altar and enter the *Capella del Rosario* (the Rosary Chapel). Learn about the victory in the famous naval Battle of Lepanto, where the Turkish advance on western Europe was halted by the combined navies of Venice, Pope Pius V, and Phillip II of Spain. End your Audio tour as you admire the Chapel's magnificent paintings by the late Renaissance artist Paolo Caliari, who was nicknamed "Veronese" for his hometown of Verona. After the final narrated tour concludes, you may retrace your steps across the alleyways of Venice as described at the beginning of this chapter or you may take Vaporetto Line 52 to return to St. Mark's Square.

SECTION 2

HISTORICAL OVERVIEW

Venice is a unique city resting on 117 islands, linked by 150 canals, and crossed by 400 bridges. Following the decline of the Roman Empire, the city was founded by mainland refugees fleeing the barbarian onslaughts, which swept across Italy in the fifth and sixth centuries. The refugees formed villages and made their living by fishing and mining the salt from the marshlands of the lagoon. Eventually, the villages banded together to form a loose, centralized government.

After being crowned Holy Roman Emperor by Pope Leo III in 800, Charlemagne tried to subdue the peoples of Northern Italy. When Charlemagne's son, Pepin, besieged the Venetian islands in 810, the communities came together against the common threat. They moved the seat of their government to a more easily-defended location called the *Rivo Alto* (the high bank) near the Rialto Bridge. The Venetians sought the protection of Constantinople, the capital of the Byzantine Empire. Charlemagne failed to take the islands and signed a treaty recognizing Venice as an ally of Byzantium. The Byzantine St. Theodore was named patron saint of Venice in deference to the city's protector.

As Venice grew to be a commercial power, Constantinople became more a business competitor than an ally. Venice's theft of the body of St. Mark the Evangelist from Egypt in 828 and the building of the magnificent St. Mark's Basilica to house the holy remains of the city's new patron saint marked the break with Constantinople. It also signaled Venice's emergence as an independent power.

From its humble beginnings in the 9th century as an exporter of salt, Venice grew to be a great commercial power and the gateway for trade between Europe and the East. Later, as its trade routes expanded, other goods—spices, jewels, rich fabrics, dyes, copper, and slaves—flowed into Venice from markets in the Orient. Venetian merchants then shipped the goods to markets throughout Western Europe. Venice also was acclaimed for its manufacture of the finest glassware. In the 15th and 16th centuries, Venice was the principal glass-producing center for all of Europe.

Venice became one of the richest cities on earth, known throughout the world as *La Serenissima Republica* (the Most Serene Republic). Although called a republic, the city was actually ruled by its wealthy elite through the

Vittore Carpaccio's *Lion of St. Mark.*

Maggior Consiglio (the Great Council), which elected its Doge — a corruption of the Latin word *dux* meaning leader. The Great Council was its chief legislative body and, after 1297, was drawn solely from patrician families listed in the *Libro d'Oro* (the Golden Book). The Senate, the judges, and the various committees handling the administration of the state, including the all-powerful Council of Ten, were drawn from the Great Council.

Venice's vast commercial fleet of merchant ships was protected by its powerful navy. The navy ships were produced in the great Arsenal of Venice, which was founded in 1104. The English word *arsenal* is derived from the Arabic word *d'arsina' a,* which means "house of industry" and was first applied to the Venetian dockyards. The Arsenal grew to employ over 16,000 workers and the navy yards covered over eighty acres at its height in the mid-16th century. Five centuries before Henry Ford created his modern assembly line and revolutionized American industrial production, the Venetian shipbuilders developed standardized parts for their galleys.

They organized each step in the construction so that separate teams would be used on each stage of the shipbuilding process. When King Henry III of France visited Venice in 1574, he was shown a keel being laid in the morning and by evening, the ship, built and fully equipped, was ready for launch. During 1570 when Cyprus was besieged by the Turks, Venice constructed a hundred new fighting ships in only two months.

After the Fourth Crusade's sack of Constantinople in 1204, in which Venice was a leading participant, Venice dominated the trade routes from the Black Sea to Palestine.

In the 13th century, Venetian merchants Nicolo and Matteo Polo extended Venice's trading routes all the way to China. They later returned to the East with Nicolo's son, Marco Polo, and spent the next 24 years in the Court of Kubla Khan, the Emperor of the Mongols. When he returned home, filled with tales of the exotic Orient, Marco Polo became known in Venice as *Marco il Milione* (Marco of the million lies). While held a prisoner of war by the Genoese, Marco dictated the tales of his adventures, which were published as the *Book of Marvels*. The book became one of the first best-sellers of the Middle Ages and ignited imaginations across Europe with its tales of the Orient's fabulous wealth.

For over a century, Venice struggled for control of the sea in a series of savage wars with the powerful Republic of Genoa. In the War of Chioggia, Genoese forces reached the very outskirts of Venice before the Venetians finally managed to decisively defeat their maritime rival in 1381.

Doge Franceco Foscari kneeling before the Lion of St. Mark on the *Porta della Carta.*

The Naval Museum's model of the Doge's ceremonial Barge, the *Bucintoro.*

With its control of the sea assured, Venice captured the Greek Peloponnesian Islands, Cyprus, and Crete. By the 16th century, Venice's maritime supremacy gave it dominance over the entire Mediterranean and control over the Adriatic, which became called the *Mare Veneziana* (the Venetian Sea).

Under the leadership of Doge Francesco Foscari, Venice turned its attention to extending its reach onto *terra firma.* Across Northern Italy, Venice took control of Verona, Vicenza, Padua, Udine, Brescia, and Bergamo. The other powers in Italy and the rest of Europe felt threatened by the increasing power of the Venetian Republic. In 1508, the League of Cambrai was formed to halt Venice's territorial advances across the Italian mainland. This unprecedented alliance pitted Venice against the combined forces of France, Spain, Hungary, Milan, Savoy, the Pope, and the Holy Roman Emperor. Through the skillful efforts of Doge Leonardo Loredan, the coalition fell apart. Pope Julius II was swayed by the arguments of Doge Loredan that the increasing threat of the Ottoman Turks, and the designs of the northern European powers on Italian territory, were the greater dangers. When the Pope switched sides and joined Venice, the fragile alliance collapsed. Venice was saved, but its expansion across Northern Italy was stopped.

The commercial power of Venice had reached its zenith. The capture of Constantinople in 1453 by the Ottoman Turks under Mehmed II ultimately led to the end of Venice's control of the seas. Venice paid substantial sums in tribute to the Sultan and entered into a series of treaties trying

Canaletto's *The Molo Looking West* (c. 1730).

to maintain her trading rights. Pope Pius II complained that commerce had turned Venice into the "Moslem's friend" to which the Venetians replied, "*Siamo Veneziani, poi Christiani*" (We are Venetians first, then Christians).

In 1499, the Ottoman Sultan slyly remarked to the Venetian Ambassador that, although their Doge was ceremoniously "wedded to the sea" each year, in the future the sea's bridegroom would be the Sultan. The Turks stood by as Venice took control of Cyprus in 1489, but then the Sultan's forces seized the island from Venice in 1500 and began marching westward, threatening the frontier of Europe.

The Turks' advance on Europe was stopped in 1571 in the climatic naval Battle of Lepanto, in which Venice played a leading role. On October 7, 1571, the combined forces of Venice, Pope Pius V, and Phillip II of Spain, led by Phillip's half brother, Don John of Austria, collided with the Turkish naval forces in the Gulf of Patras near Lepanto. In the fierce hand-to-hand fighting, some 9,000 Christians and 20,000 Turks were killed, and 117 Turkish galleys were sunk or captured. The victory was greeted with wild celebrations throughout Europe. The large Venetian contingent was led by Sebastiano Venier, who later served Venice as Doge.

Canaletto's *Riva degli Schiavoni Looking East* (c. 1730).

Despite the victory in the Battle of Lepanto, Venice's days as a dominant commercial power were numbered. The Turkish forces regrouped and continued to skirmish with Venice off and on for another century. Little by little, Venice's eastern possessions were swallowed up by the Turks, and her trade routes were blocked. The discoveries in the New World by Christopher Columbus, and the explorations around the Horn of Africa by Vasco da Gama, led to the development of alternate trade routes that bypassed the Turkish threat and the former Venetian monopoly. The flood of gold from the New World further contributed to the erosion of Venice's prosperity.

By the end of the 16th century, Venice was no longer a great power on the world scene. With the emergence of the new European nations, the center of gravity for military and economic power shifted to the mainland countries. The Venetians continued to live in the splendid isolation of their beautiful city with their colorful pageants and great public processions, but the people grew complacent and no longer had the will to play a major role in world affairs. Venice's government grew stagnant and corrupt.

When Napoleon's forces threatened to capture Venice, the Great Council met and voted to dissolve the Republic. On May 17, 1797, Doge

Lodovico Manin, the 120th and final Doge of the Republic, meekly stepped down, thus ending almost a thousand years of Venice's independence as a state. When the French forces took control of Venice, Napoleon ordered the burning of the great Arsenal. The Doge's huge and richly gilded ceremonial barge — the last *Bucintoro* — was sunk. The symbols of the Republic were stripped from public buildings, the Treasury of St. Mark was plundered, and numerous churches, monasteries, and *scuole* were closed. Many of the city's greatest paintings and sculptures were taken as trophies back to Paris.

Statue of Victor Emmanuel II, the first King of a united Italy.

Napoleon ceded Venice by treaty to his old foe, Austria, in the Treaty of Campo Formio in October 1797. In 1803, Venice was recovered by Napoleon and made a part of the Kingdom of Italy. Napoleon proclaimed himself Emperor of France and King of Italy. He appointed his stepson Eugène de Beauharnais Viceroy of Italy. After Napoleon's defeat at Waterloo in 1815, Venice and her possessions on the mainland were ceded to the Austrians following the Congress of Vienna.

Under Austrian occupation, Venice's port was extended and a railway bridge was built over the lagoon linking Venice to the mainland. In 1848, the people of Venice rebelled and briefly gained independence from Austrian rule. The popular Daniele Manin was proclaimed President of the New Republic of Venice. The Austrians counterattacked and laid siege to Venice. Just a year later, in 1849, after months of starvation, bombardment, and weakened by an outbreak of cholera, the city surrendered. The Austrians held power until 1866, when Venice joined the other Italian states to form a united Kingdom of Italy under Victor Emmanuel II.

In 1895, the first International Art Exhibition was held in Venice.

During the winter floods of *acque alte* (high water), ramps are placed all along St. Mark's Square to allow tourists to visit St. Mark's and the adjacent stores and cafés.

Known as the *Biennale*, it is held every other year and has grown to become a showplace for the latest developments in modern art. The nearby *Lido* was developed into a popular seaside retreat for wealthy Europeans.

World Wars I and II left Venice largely unscathed. Venice was liberated on April 28, 1944, even though the fighting continued around nearby Padua for another month.

On the third and fourth of November, 1966, a combination of heavy rains, high tides, and gale force winds blowing from the south caused the waters of the Adriatic to surge over the banks of the canals into the streets and squares of Venice and into St. Mark's Basilica itself. The water, polluted with oil and waste, rose to a record level of six and a half feet above sea level and stayed at that height for 24 long hours causing incalculable damage to homes, shops, churches, and palaces. It took many years for Venice to recover, but the tragedy ignited worldwide concern over Venice's future and galvanized support for the restoration of Venice and its artworks.

The *acque alte* (high water) is increasingly troublesome during the winter months and water frequently floods St. Mark's Square and its nearby buildings. There are proposals to build a series of flood barriers that

View across St. Mark's Square towards the basilica.

could be raised to block off the lagoon's entrance to the sea if a storm surge threatens the city. London, Rotterdam, and Hamburg have installed similar barriers, but Venice's plans have been mired in bureaucratic and political bickering. With global warming and rising water levels, Venice's survival for future generations will be precarious.

Today, the flood of tourists poses an even greater challenge to Venice. Over twelve million people visit Venice each year, taxing the city's resources to the limit. There have been various proposals to limit the number of tourists by charging an entry fee or moving to a reservation system, but these have so far proved unworkable or ineffective.

The cost of living in the city of Venice is much higher than elsewhere in Italy and there are few opportunities for employment other than the tourist industry. In 1945, there were over 178,000 people living in Venice. Today, there are fewer than 70,000. Venice's population continues to dwindle as young Venetians move to the mainland in search of better jobs and more affordable housing.

Even though it faces many modern problems, Venice remains one of the most enchanting cities in the world for travelers. The city's rich history

Masked revelers at *Carnevale*.

is kept alive in the various festivals and regattas that the city hosts through-out the year. In 1979, Venice revived its famous celebration of *Carnivale* that had been outlawed by Napoleon. The term *Carnivale* was derived from the Latin *carne vale* (farewell to meat), as Christians celebrated in the weeks before *Martedi Grasso* (Fat Tuesday) and the beginning of the solemn season of Lent. Venice's celebration of *Carnivale*, begun in the 11th century, reached its heyday in the early 18th century, when the fes-tivities lasted for nearly two months of unrestrained revelry. Today, Venice swarms with costumed partygoers for ten days of festivities before Lent, ending with fabulous masked balls for the *glitterati* and dancing in St. Mark's Square.

On Ascension Day, May 19th of each year, Venice celebrates its sym-bolic wedding to the sea—a ceremony dating back to the conquest of the Dalmatian pirates by the Doge Pietro Orseolo II. The Doge, the clergy, and the dignitaries would lead the procession on the *Bucintoro*. The Patriarch of Venice blessed the sea with holy water and the Doge threw a golden ring into the sea saying, "As a token of eternal rule we marry you, oh sea." The city still reenacts this ancient ceremony with full pomp and pageantry.

The popular *Festa del Redentore* (the Feast of the Redeemer), in which the people of Venice celebrate the city's deliverance from the great plague of 1576, is still held between the third Saturday and Sunday of each July. Each year a pontoon bridge is built over the canal so that the people of Venice can cross over the temporary bridge to attend mass at the beautiful *Il Redentore* (Church of the Redeemer), designed by Andrea Palladio. All weekend long, the canal is crowded with boats of all shapes and sizes, filled with groups waiting for the spectacular fireworks display presented on Saturday night.

On November 21st of each year, Venice celebrates the *Festa della Salute* (the Feast of St. Mary of Health) to celebrate its deliverance from the plague of 1630. Each year, a temporary pontoon bridge is constructed linking the banks of the Grand Canal, and grateful worshipers walk over the bridge to light candles in the *Chiesa di Santa Maria della Salute* (the Church St. Mary of Health) to commemorate the end of the plague and to pray for good health in the coming year.

Venice's most famous regatta is the *Regata Storica* (the Historical Regatta), which takes place on the first Sunday of September. In the Historical Regatta, gondoliers and their boats compete in various events. The colorful event starts off with a magnificent procession of boats, their oarsmen in full historical regalia.

Scene from the historical reenactment of the Rescue of the Maidens before the start of *Carnivale*.

SECTION 3

PLANNING YOUR TRIP

When planning your trip, you should check the opening and closing times listed in Section 10 of this guide for general guidance. Remember! Opening and closing times often vary with the season and change with little notice. The entrance fees to museums and churches continually change. The author and publisher have tried to confirm the most current data prior to publication, but try to reconfirm the opening and closing times when you arrive.

Before you leave home, you can check for current information on opening and closing times and admission fees on one of the recommended Venice Web sites listed in this guide such as www.aguestinvenice.com. This is the new English online version of the helpful tourist guide *Ospite di Venezia* (A Guest In Venice). The *Ospite di Venezia* Web site provides the most up-to-date information about current art exhibitions, music, opera and theater performances, films, lectures, conferences, sports, and other events in Venice. It also offers helpful information on transportation schedules and fares, hotels, restaurants, and shops. When you get to Venice, you should pick up a hard copy of the latest *Ospite di Venezia* (A Guest in Venice) at one of the Venice tourist offices at the train station or the airport, or ask for a copy at your hotel.

While in Venice, look for the Venice tourist office, the *Azienda di Promozione Turistica*, called the "APT." The main office is located at the Venice Pavilion on the waterfront just past the *San Marco Vallaresso* Vaporetto landing, which is near the *Giardinetti ex Reali* (the Royal Gardens). The Venice Pavilion APT has a bookstore stocked with local travel literature, and sells tickets for upcoming concerts, exhibitions, and local events. The APT also publishes its own magazine, *Leo*, which includes interesting articles about cultural events and updates on what is happening in the city. Other smaller APT tourist offices can be found at the Santa Lucia train station, the Marco Polo International airport, on the nearby

The Venice Pavilion by the *Giardinetti ex Reali* (the Royal Gardens).

The Royal Gardens pictured with the Bell Tower of St. Mark *(behind)* and Venice's Mint *(right)*.

island of the *Lido*, and in the city of Venice at 71 *Calle dell' Ascensione*, which can be found just off *Piazza San Marco* (St. Mark's Square). The Venice tourist offices are open daily from 9:00 a.m. to 5:30 p.m. Telephone: (041) 522 5150.

The city offers two types of combination tickets for admission to a number of the city's most important museums. The Museum Card allows entry to the *Musei di Piazza San Marco* (the Museums of St. Mark's Square), which are the Doge's Palace, the Correr Museum, the Archeological Museum, and the Monuments Hall at the Library of St. Mark. You cannot buy separate tickets to these sites. The Museum Card costs €9,50 and admission is valid for 3 months so you can make return visits to the sites if you have more time to explore.

The Museum Pass allows entry to the Museums of St. Mark's Square, plus it includes admission to the Museums of 18th Century Culture, *Ca' Rezzonico, Casa Goldoni*, and *Palazzo Mocenigo*. The Museum Pass is also good for admission to the museums on the islands of *Burano, Murano*, and *Torcello*. You may choose to buy separate admission tickets to *Ca' Rezzonico, Casa Goldoni, Palazzo Mocenigo,* and the island Museums. The Museum Pass costs €15,50 and admission is valid for 3 months. If you have a few days in Venice and plan to visit the Museums of St. Mark's Square and at least *Ca' Rezzonico*, then you might want to go ahead and buy the Museum Pass.

If you have *less* than a full day to explore Venice, you should treat yourself to the unforgettable view offered by taking Vaporetto Line 1 down the Grand Canal and then take the first four Tours found on Tracks 1, 2, 3, and 4 of CD One, which explore St. Mark's Square and the exterior of St. Mark's Basilica, the interior of St. Mark's Basilica, the exterior of the Doge's Palace, the Bell Tower of St. Mark's, and the surrounding area. The leisurely ride down the Grand Canal on Vaporetto Line 1 offers the best overall introduction to Venice as the boat glides past picture-perfect views of the many Gothic palaces that line the crowded waterway of this unique city. Get off at the *San Marco Vallaresso* Vaporetto landing, which is near the *Giardinetti ex Reali* (the Royal Gardens). Walk over to St. Mark's Square, where the first tour found on Track 1 of CD One begins. If the inevitable line of people waiting to get into St. Mark's is too long, you might postpone taking the second tour, which explores the interior of the basilica. You can go on to the other tours and then return later in the day to explore the interior of St. Mark's in Tour 2 found on Track 2 of CD One. If the line to enter St. Mark's is short, you might want to listen to the introduction on Track 1 and then skip to Track 2 to explore the interior before it gets too crowded.

After you have enjoyed the sights along the Grand Canal, and taken the first four tours found on Tracks 1, 2, 3, and 4 of CD One, then catch Vaporetto Line 1 or 82 and go back up the Grand Canal to enjoy the rich art treasures and see the tombs of many famous Venetians in the *Basilica di Santa Maria Gloriosa dei Frari* (Basilica of St. Mary in Glory of the Brothers) discussed on Tour 8 found on Track 8 of CD Two. Get off at the *San Toma* Vaporetto landing. For the first-time visitor who is pressed for

time, the first four tours found on Tracks 1 through 4 of CD One and Tour 8 found on Track 8 of CD Two will give you the best overview of Venice's long history and essential artistic highlights that should not be missed!

If you have a full day in Venice, you might take the first four tours on Tracks 1 through 4 of CD One. After that, you might stroll down Venice's beautiful waterfront promenade, listening to Tour 5 found on Track 5 of CD One. On Tour 5 you will visit the *Chiesa di San Zaccaria* (the Church of St. Zacharias) and then end at the *Chiesa di Santa Maria della*

Side view of St. Mark's Basilica.

Visitazione (the Church of the Pieta). You might then catch Vaporetto Line 1 or 82 to go visit the Church of the Frari. Conclude your day wandering through the colorful market area near the Rialto Bridge, which is discussed in Tour 10 found on Track 10 of CD Two. If you still have time, you could hop on a Vaporetto and visit one or more of the other sites that interest you that are mentioned in this guide.

You might wish to take in an evening concert at the *Chiesa di Santa Maria della Visitazione* (the Church of the Pieta). You can reserve concert tickets on-line at the Web site listed in the guide, or you can pur-

Sansovino's bronze statue by the entrance of the *Loggetta*.

chase your tickets at the ticket window located just inside the vestibule of the Church of the Pieta or at the APT Venice tourist office in the Venice Pavilion found near the *Giardinetti ex Reali* (the Royal Gardens).

If you are trying to see as much of Venice as possible during your visit, you should remember that most churches are closed during the middle of the day. The *Basilica di Santa Maria Gloriosa dei Frari* (Basilica of St. Mary in Glory of the Brothers) and St. Mark's Basilica are generally open all day and stay open much later, than most other sites. You may want to go to one of the art museums such as the *Gallerie dell' Accademia* (the Academy Museum), *Museo del Settecento Veneziano* (Museum of the Venetian 18th Century), housed in the elegant *Ca' Rezzonico*, or the *Museo Civico Correr* (the Correr Museum), which are open during mid-day. The story of the gondola discussed at the Orseolo Basin in Tour 9 found on Track 9 of CD Two, and the exploration of the Rialto Bridge and the Church of St. James and the colorful market areas discussed in Tour 10 found on Track 10 of CD Two can be done during mid-day or in the early evening when other sites are closed.

The twelve narrated tours in this guide can be completed in two or three days, depending on the crowds, or you can move at a more leisurely pace, and take time out for lunch at a nearby *trattoria* or sit at an outdoor café sipping a glass of wine while enjoying the passing parade of tourists from around the world. Remember, the prices for food and drink are the most expensive in the restaurants closest to St. Mark's Square. The prices drop somewhat as you get off the beaten track and into the less touristy areas, but prices are generally higher in Venice than elsewhere in Italy. Seafood is the specialty of Venetian restaurants and should not be missed.

The narrated tours in this guide do not cover the lavish interior rooms of the *Palazzo Ducale* (the Doge's Palace). If you are staying in Venice for several days, or have been to Venice before and have seen the other main sites, you should definitely find time to visit the many grand public rooms and private apartments of the Doge's Palace and its prisons. For a first-time visitor, or if you only have a limited amount of time in Venice, the endless parade of grand public rooms can be a bit overwhelming, and the other sites covered in this Audio CD Guide would provide a better overview of the city.

The Doge's Palace, a beautiful example of Venetian Gothic architecture, is the combined residence of the Doges, the assembly halls of the *Maggior Consiglio* (the Great Council), the law courts and its prison. The Palace was begun as a fortress in the 9th century, and was rebuilt and expanded many times before taking on its current form in the 14th and 15th centuries. In the

center of the Doge's Palace is a courtyard built in a classic Renaissance style with a grand staircase, where the Doges of Venice were crowned. It is known as the *Scala dei Giganti* (Stairway of the Giants) and was built in the 15th century by Antonio Rizzo. Looming at the top of the stairs are two oversized statues sculpted by Jacopo Sansovino in 1567. The figures of Mars on the left and Neptune on the right symbolized Venice's dominance over the land and the sea.

The Doge's Palace is accessible only with either the Museum Pass or

The courtyard of the Doge's Palace.

View of the beautiful Venetian Gothic façade of the Doge's Palace.

the Museum Card. The admission to the Doge's Palace allows access to the private apartments of the Doges and the public rooms, each larger and more splendidly appointed than the last. For a small additional fee, you can rent an audio guide of the Doge's Palace, or you can wander on your own through the series of rooms along the marked route, which will take you to the enormous *Sala del Maggior Consiglio* (Hall of the Great Council) where the members of the Great Council assembled. This cavernous assembly room is dominated by Domenico and Jacopo Tintoretto's huge painting of *Paradise.* Measuring 25 by 81 feet, it is one of the largest paintings in the world. On the ceiling of the huge hall is Veronese's *Apotheosis of Venice* and other panels glorifying the Venetian Republic.

The route for the self-guided tour leads off from the hall of the Great Council through a series of passageways and stairs, then across the Bridge of Sighs to the 16th century prisons known as the *Prigioni Nuove* (New Prisons). The path then returns again to the Doge's Palace, ending in the beautiful Renaissance courtyard.

You will find the entrance to the ticket desk for the Doge's Palace on the waterfront opposite the granite column topped by the winged lion of St. Mark. Check inside at the ticket desk for the times when the English guided tours of the *Itinerari Segreti* (the Secret Trails) are being offered. The English tours of the Secret Trails are generally given during the summer months at 10:00 a.m. and noon. This fascinating guided tour takes you through back halls and passageways to rooms not seen on the main tour routes. The tour includes the offices of the private secretaries of the Great Council and the law courts, the torture chamber used to extract confessions from criminals and enemies of the state, and the cell where Casanova was imprisoned. The guided *Itinerari Segreti* tour gives you an intriguing glimpse into the inner workings of the Venetian government. After the tour, you can wander through the rest of the Doge's Palace or pick up the audio self-guided tour.

Doge's Palace

Admission charge; Open Monday - Sunday 9:00 a.m. - 7:00 p.m. (April 1 until October 31); 9:00 a.m. - 5:00 p.m. (November 1 until March 31)

If your time permits, you really should consider visiting the *Galleria dell' Accademia* (the Academy Museum), which can be reached by Vaporetto Lines 1 or 82. Get off at the *Accademia* Vaporetto landing. Since 1807, the Academy Museum has been housed in the former church of *Santa Maria della Carità*, its convent, and the adjacent *Scuola della Carità*. It offers the world's most comprehensive collection of Venetian School paintings from the 15th to the 18th centuries. Napoleon closed many churches and monasteries and gathered their displaced artworks here to augment the holdings of the Academy of Fine Arts, which had been founded by Giovanni Battista Piazzetta.

The Academy Museum offers an excellent audio guide that examines its rich holdings, which are laid out in chronological order from the 15th to the 18th centuries. Since it is open late, you might decide to end your day in Venice enjoying the museum's collection of masterpieces by Bellini, Giorgione, Tintoretto, Titian, and Veronese.

Academy Museum

Admission charge; Open Monday 9:00 a.m. - 2:00 p.m., Tuesday - Sunday 8:15 a.m. - 7:15 p.m.

View of the *Gallerie dell' Accademia* (the Academy Museum).

The *Museo Civico Correr* (the Correr Museum) is located on St. Mark's Square in the second floor of the Napoleonic Wing. This museum, dedicated to Venetian history, was begun in 1830 with a bequest by Teodoro Correr. Correr had collected objects of the old Republic that had survived Napoleonic and Austrian rule. The museum contains a fascinating collection of historical artifacts from the old Venetian Republic, including articles worn by the Doge, artifacts from the period of Napoleonic rule, the Austrian occupation and Venice's unification with Italy. The Museum also holds many works by Venetian artists, including Giovanni and Gentile Bellini, Vittore Carpaccio, Jacopo Sansovino, and Antonio Canova, as well as works by Flemish artists, such as Pieter Bruegel, Hugo van der Goes, and Dirk Bouts.

Correr Museum
Admission charge; Open daily from 9:00 a.m. until 7:00 p.m.
(April 1 until October 31) and from 9:00 a.m. until 5:00 p.m.
(November 1 until March 31)

The *Museo del Settecento Veneziano* (Museum of the Venetian 18th Century), housed in the elegant *Ca' Rezzonico*, has reopened after a long period of restoration. *Ca' Rezzonico* is located on the Grand Canal on

91

View from the gallery of St. Mark's of the Napoleonic Wing with the Correr Museum.

Fondamenta Rezzonico near *Campo San Barbara* (St. Barbara Square). Take Vaporetto Line 1 and get off at the *Rezzonico* Vaporetto landing.

This extravagant palace contains ornate period furniture, superb works of art by Francesco Guardi, Canaletto, Pietro Longhi, and fabulous ceiling frescoes by Giambattista Tiepolo and others. The palace was designed by Baldassare Longhena. Construction was completed under Giorgio Massari. The palace was bought as a showplace by the nouveau riche Rezzonico family, who bought their way into the aristocracy during the decline of the Venetian Republic. The Museum offers a detailed audio guide that explores the many treasures of the palace. It also has a modern café and a pleasant garden.

Museum of the Venetian 18th Century
Admission charge; Open Wednesday - Monday 10:00 a.m. - 5:00 p.m.

The *Museo Storico Navale* (Museum of Naval History) offers visitors a welcome break from churches, palaces, and Madonna-filled museums. It is only a few minutes walk down the waterfront promenade, *Riva degli Schiavoni,* proceeding away from the Doge's Palace. The museum can also be reached by Vaporetto on Lines 1 or 52. Get off at the *Arsenale* landing, if you are using Line 1, or the *Tana* landing, if you are using Line 52.

Despite its dreary exterior, this museum offers interesting exhibits depicting the history of the Venetian Republic era and the Italian Navy. The Museum's exhibits range from small scale model boats to artifacts from historical vessels that have been recovered. Don't miss the model

Entrance to Museum of Naval History.

of the Doge's gilded ceremonial barge, the *Bucintoro*, used by the Doge to celebrate the annual *Sposalizio del Mare*, (ceremonial marriage of Venice with the sea). The nearby Ships Pavilion houses a large collection of Venetian boats, including many of the elaborate gondolas and boats used in the city's historical regattas.

Museum of Naval History

Admission charge; Open Monday - Saturday 8:45 a.m. - 1:30 p.m.

Arsenal Gate built in 1460 by Antonio Gambello.

Just down from the Naval Museum you can find the Renaissance gateway, with its two massive towers protecting the entrance to the Arsenal. It was built by Antonio Gambello in 1460 in the style of a Roman triumphal arch. The *Arsenale* is now an Italian Navy yard and is closed to the public, but the gateway is worth the short walk. The lion on the left and the large reclining lion to the right were taken from the Greek port of Piraeus in 1692, while the two smaller lions are from the Greek island of Delos.

If modern art interests you, then you should try to find time to explore the Peggy Guggenheim Collection. It is housed in the beautiful 18th century *Palazzo Venier dei Leoni* (Venier Palace of the Lions) along the Grand Canal near the *Chiesa di Santa Maria della Salute* (the Church of St. Mary of Health). It can be reached by Vaporetto on Line 1. Get off at the *Salute* landing. Turn to the right after you disembark from the Vaporetto, cross the small bridge, and follow the signs.

The collection offers the public a wide range of modern art, including works by Picasso, Pollock, Kandinsky, and Brancusi. Don't miss Marino Marini's statue *Angelo della Citta* (Angel of the Citadel) in the garden.

Guggenheim Collection
Admission charge; Open Wednesday - Monday 10:00 a.m. - 6:00 p.m.

If you have time and want to explore the wealth of art contained in Venice's many beautiful churches, the Venice tourist office sells a Chorus

Venier Palace of the Lions housing the Guggenheim Collection.

Pass that allows entry to the *Basilica Santa Maria Gloriosa dei Frari* (Basilica of St. Mary in Glory of the Brothers) and fourteen of Venice's less frequently visited churches. The Chorus Pass is also sold in the churches covered in the program. The Chorus Pass is good for one year with the proceeds going towards the restoration and upkeep of these historic churches. For an extra fee, audio tapes with detailed narratives are available at many of the churches visited on the Chorus Pass. Unless you are planning on visiting four or more churches, it would

Church of the Madonna of the Garden.

be less expensive to pay the admission to the churches separately.

The *Chiesa di Madonna dell'Orto* (the Church of the Madonna of the Garden) with its wonderful works by Tintoretto is highly recommended. The church can be reached on Vaporetto Lines 51 or 52. Get off at the *dell'Orto* landing. This parish church, with its distinctive onion-domed bell tower is named for the miraculous statue of the Madonna that was found in a nearby garden (*orto* in Italian). The church is filled with many works by Tintoretto, who is buried in the chapel to the right of the high altar. See his powerful *Last Judgment* and *Adoration of the Golden Calf.*

Church of the Madonna of the Garden
Admission charge; Open Monday - Saturday 10:00 a. m. - 5:00 p.m., Sunday 1:00 p.m. - 5:00 p.m.

Fans of Tintoretto also will not want to miss the *Scuola Grande di San Rocco* (the School of St. Roch). It is located just behind the rear of the *Basilica Santa Maria Gloriosa dei Frari* (Basilica of St. Mary in Glory of the Brothers) explored in Tour 8. The *scuola* was dedicated to San Rocco (St. Roch), who was venerated as a protector against the plague. The *scuola* features two entire floors of Tintoretto's works. In the upper hall are paintings depicting scenes from the life of Christ and in the lower hall are paintings based on the life of the Virgin. The *scuola's* other fine paintings include works by Titian, Tiepolo, and Giorgione. The upper hall is also justly famous for the elaborately carved benches by Francesco Pianta completed in the late 17th century. Be sure to see Tintoretto's *St. Roch in Glory* and his stunning *Crucifixion* in the *Sala dell' Albergo* in the upper hall.

School of St. Roch

Admission charge; Open from March 28 to November 2, 9:00 a.m. - 5.30 p.m. on all days; open from November to February, Monday to Friday 10:00 a.m. - 1:00 p.m., and Saturday and Sunday 10:00 a.m. - 4:00 p.m.; open during Christmas week and Carnival week 10:00 a.m. - 4:00 p.m.

If you want to see the famed Venetian glass blowers in action you can visit the factories on the nearby island of Murano. (See the directions given in Practical Information pages 107-108). Or, if you are pressed for time, there is a daily exhibition of glass blowing given in the Palazzo Trevisan, which is located just behind St. Mark's Basilica. Walk down the *Piazzetta dei Leoncini* (Little Square of the Lions) away from St. Mark's Square on the north side of the basilica and cross the bridge to Palazzo Trevisan.

Whether you only have one afternoon or an entire week to see Venice, there is never enough time to see it all. When planning your trip, remember that Venice is much more than its fabulous churches, extraordinary museums, and ornate palaces. Be sure to take time out to wander off the main tourist paths. It is a marvelous place to simply walk around and drink in the atmospheric sights, smells, and sounds. Around any corner you may find the striking façade of a Gothic palace or an old stone bridge over a charming canal lined with boats. Venice is a magical city you can return to many times and there will always be new treasures waiting to be discovered and enjoyed.

SECTION 4

A WORD ABOUT GONDOLAS

Virgin of the Gondoliers found at the *Ponte della Paglia* (the Bridge of Straw).

While in Venice, you should consider pampering yourself with a gondola ride. A gondola ride is not cheap, but the experience is one you will never forget, and it allows you to encounter Venice as it was meant to be seen. Go ahead and splurge. Enjoy one of those once-in-a-lifetime magical experiences. The narration in Tour 9 found on Track 9 of CD Two discusses the history of the gondola and explains the symbolism of its traditional decorations.

Gondola excursions can be booked through your hotel. You also can make your arrangements directly at the Orseolo Basin, where many gondoliers gather, or at various gondola stands around the city. As you walk in the main tourist areas past the flotillas of parked boats, you may be approached with polite offers of "Gondola?" or when business is slow, a gondolier may call out to you as you walk by. When choosing a proposed route, remember: although it is lined with beautiful palazzos, the Grand Canal is the freeway of Venice. It is usually very busy and can be quite choppy. Before agreeing to any excursion, be reasonably sure that you are near the area you want to explore by gondola, or you will waste precious time getting away from the hectic main tourist areas to that quiet canal of your dreams. Enjoy the crowded Grand Canal by the cheaper Vaporetti and save your gondola ride for the quieter, picturesque interior canals, where you will have a smoother ride and a more romantic experience.

The typical price is for the entire gondola excursion and is not based on how many passengers are enjoying the ride. Gondolas normally hold up to five passengers, although the gondolier may agree to six, especially if some of the passengers are children. Do not expect the gondolier to sing. Musical accompaniment is usually extra.

The official rates, which are often ignored, start at €62,00 for the first 50-minute gondola ride, and €31,00 for each additional 25 minutes thereafter. For nighttime service (after 8:00 p.m.), the base rate goes up. Pick up a copy of the current *Ospite di Venezia* (A Guest in Venice) at one of the Venice tourist offices or from your hotel to check the latest official price schedule. Free market capitalism has had a hold on Venice for over a thousand years, and the actual rates quoted by the gondolier may be more in high season, depending on supply and demand. At least you can use the "official fare" as the baseline

A gondola ride through the quiet back canals of Venice.

in negotiations for your fare. The clerk at your hotel would probably be able to make the arrangements for a gondola ride for you.

The crowded Grand Canal is the freeway of Venice.

You can find gondola stands at the Orseolo Basin, as described in Tour 9; in front of the Hotel Danieli on the *Riva degli Schiavoni*; near *Calle Vallaresso* in front of Harry's Bar; on the Grand Canal outside of Venice's *Santa Lucia* train station; near the *Piazzale Roma* Vaporetto landing; along the waterfront by the Doge's Palace; by the *San Sofia* Vaporetto landing; by the *San Toma* Vaporetto landing; near *Campo San Moise*; and near the Rialto Bridge along the *Riva Carbon*.

Traghetto ferrying passengers across a foggy Grand Canal.

Make sure that you and the gondolier have agreed on the length of the ride, so that the agreed price is just that. When you've reached a full, firm price, board the gondola and enjoy your journey. When you are through, no additional tip is required or expected, although the gondolier certainly would not object if you are overcome with generosity.

If you want to say that you have ridden in a gondola, but the budget will simply not allow for it, the closest experience to a gondola ride is the *Traghetto*, a public ferry, which carries pedestrians across the Grand Canal at various points along the Grand Canal. The *Traghetti* are similar to privately rented gondolas, but you will pay only a fraction of the price to enjoy the short ride across the Grand Canal. Follow the *Traghetti* signs, down to the water where you will see the waiting gondola. *Traghetti* crossings can be found near the Vaporetto landings of *San Maria del Giglio; San Barnaba; San Toma; Riva Carbon; San Sofia; San Marcuola;* and the *Ferrovia*. The ride across the Canal is usually short, but the brief experience can be great fun. Although you will see that it is customary among native Venetians to stand up while crossing the canal, you may wish to sit down and hold on to your belongings during the crossing, unless you have exceptionally good balance.

SECTION 5

PRACTICAL INFORMATION ON VAPORETTI (VENICE'S WATERBUS SYSTEM)

How to Use the Vaporetti System

Getting around in Venice is part of the fun of exploring this wonderful city. No cars or bicycles are allowed in Venice. The convenient waterbus system is the primary means of transportation through the network of canals and waterways, which take the place of streets. The larger motorboats you will be using to get around for these twelve tours are called *Vaporetti* (little steamers). The sleeker, and somewhat faster, boats you may see are called *Motoscafi*. These are often used to reach the outlying islands of *Murano, Burano,* and *Torcello.*

The Venice transportation service is the *Azienda del Consorzio Trasporti Veneziano,* better known as the ACTV. The ACTV transportation service Web site is very easy to navigate and its Web address is listed in the guide's section "Venice Web Sites." Click on the site map at the ACTV Web site and follow the directions to explore the waterbus system and the stops along its routes.

The various Vaporetti lines make stops all along the Grand Canal and ply the waters around Venice. Several lines go on to the outlying islands of the *Lido, Murano, Burano,* and *Torcello* in the lagoon. The boats run almost constantly up and down the Grand Canal, so you will seldom have to wait more than a few minutes for one to come along. The main routes are serviced until early evening. There is reduced service in the evening. If you find yourself waiting for over 20 minutes, check at the ticket booth to see if there is some problem, or an unexpected strike.

You can catch a Vaporetto at various landing docks that are located at

different points along the canals. They are clearly marked with the official yellow ACTV signs and the name of the landing. Tickets are usually available at the booth outside the landing, or they

Covered landing dock just past the ticket booth, where you will wait for your Vaporetto.

Typical ticket booth.

can be purchased at shops and tobacco stands that display the ACTV sign. You can always purchase a ticket on board the boat from the crew, but make sure you buy the ticket immediately upon boarding. If you are caught without a validated ticket, you will be fined on the spot.

Under ACTV's new procedures, the tickets are now validated and time stamped when sold. If your ticket has not been validated, you will need to insert your ticket into the yellow ticket machine located on the landing, which will date and time stamp the ticket. If you want to buy multiple single tickets for future use, you will have to ask that they not be pre-validated when you purchase your advance tickets.

The standard ticket is good for one trip with no breaks in your journey. There are special discount tickets for family groups. If you will be in Venice for an entire day or longer, you might want to buy one of the special 24-hour or 72-hour tickets that are available for individuals and groups.

Indicator boards for Lines 1, 82, and N, the nighttime service route.

Check the current fares in the latest issue of *Ospite di Venezia* (A Guest in Venice). Before you leave on vacation, you can check for current fares at the easy-to-navigate ACTV Web site or the Guest in Venice Web site listed in this guide. These multi-hour tickets allow unlimited travel on the major lines. You will then be free to hop on and off the boats as often as you like and will not have to worry about the ticket.

On the wall in the covered landing dock, you will find a yellow indicator board identifying the different Vaporetto lines that stop there. The indicator board also will list the names of each of the landings where the boat will make a short stop along its route. Each landing along the Grand Canal, and in the outly-ing areas, is clearly marked with its name. The boatman usually announces the name of the upcoming landing as the boat approaches each dock, so that you can move to the side of the Vaporetto towards the landing where you will disembark. The newer Vaporetti have electronic boards that dis-play the name of the next stop. Since the same landings are used for boats heading in both directions, it is helpful to watch the boat as it approaches to make sure it is going in the direction that you are headed. When in doubt, ask the boatman *"Per San Marco?"* or just mention the name of whatever destination you are seeking. It is always better to be safe and ask, rather than head in the wrong direction on an unexpected adventure.

Upon arriving in Venice by train, most visitors catch Vaporetto Line 1 to make their journey down the Grand Canal towards St. Mark's Square at the *Ferrovia* Vaporetto landing. You will find the *Ferrovia* Vaporetto land-ing just outside the *Santa Lucia* train station. As you exit down the steps from the train station, you will be facing the Grand Canal. The ticket booth and landing for Vaporetto Line 1, marked with a yellow sign *Ferrovia,* will be just down on your right. The Vaporetto landing and ticket booth for Line 82 will be down on the left as you exit the train station. Vaporetto Line 1 is generally very crowded. When you board the boat, try to get a seat outside near the bow. The views are excellent on either side. As passengers in the seats ahead of you disembark, you might be able to work yourself up towards the front of the boat for the best view.

VAPORETTO LINES AND STOPS

The primary Vaporetti Lines you will use to visit the sights described in this guide are Lines 1, 82, and 52. Although Line 1 is called the *"Accelerato,"* it is actually the "local" and makes all the stops along the Grand Canal, from *Piazzale Roma,* the main parking lot, to the *Lido,* its last stop. Line 1 begins at *Piazzale Roma,* the boat landing for the main Venice car park and the drop-off point for those arriving by bus from the airport. The next landing reached by Line 1 is *Ferrovia,* which is the boat landing for those arriving at the *Santa Lucia* train station. The sixth stop is at *Ca' d'Oro,* where you can get off to visit the *Ca' d'Oro / Galleria Franchetti*

View of the Vaporetto landing at *Piazzale Roma* just past the bus drop off.

(House of Gold and Franchetti Gallery). The seventh stop is the *Rialto,* where you will begin your exploration of the Rialto Bridge, the church of *San Giacomo di Rialto* (St. James of the Rialto), and the surrounding area discussed in Tour 10 found on Track 10 of CD Two. The tenth landing reached on Line 1 is *San Toma,* where you will disembark to begin your exploration of the Church of the Frari, discussed in Tour 8 found on Track 8 of CD Two. The next stop is *Ca' Rezzonico,* where you can visit the *Museo del Settecento Veneziano* (Museum of the Venetian 18th Century) housed in the *Ca' Rezzonico.* Next comes the *Accademia* landing, where you may stop to visit the famed *Galleria dell' Accademia* (the Academy Museum). Two stops later, you will come to *Salute,* where you can disembark to begin your exploration of *Chiesa di Santa Maria della Salute* (the Church St. Mary of Health), and the *Dogana di Mare* (Venice's Customhouse), as discussed in Tour 11 found on Track 11 of CD Two. *Salute* is also the best landing to reach the Peggy Guggenheim Collection. After the *Salute,* you will come to the *Vallaresso* landing also called *San Marco Vallaresso,* even though the signs merely say *Vallaresso. Vallaresso* is the correct landing to get off to begin your exploration of St. Mark's Square, St. Mark's Basilica, and the Doge's Palace, which are discussed in Tours 1 through 5 found on Tracks 1 through 5 of CD One.

Indicator Board for Line 1 showing the stops made by the Vaporetto all along the Grand Canal.

If you missed getting off at the *San Marco Vallaresso* landing, do not worry. After stopping at the *San Marco Vallaresso* landing, Line 1 continues on to *San Zaccaria,* which can be an alternate landing for beginning Tours 1 through 4. It is also the landing where you may begin your exploration of the *Riva degli Schiavoni*, Venice's waterfront promenade, with the *Chiesa di San Zaccaria* (the Church of St. Zacharias), *Chiesa di Santa Maria della Visitazione* (the Church of the Pieta), covered in Tour 5 found on Track 5 of CD One, and the *Scuola di San Giorgio Schiavoni* (the School of St. George of the Dalmatians), discussed on Tour 6 found on Track 6 of CD Two. The next stop is *Arsenale*, where you can get off to see the monumental gateway to Venice's Arsenal, which is now a navy shipyard and the *Museo Storico Navale* (the Museum of Navel History). Before heading across the bay, the Line 1 Vaporetto stops at *Giardini*, which is Venice's largest garden, and usually there are no tourists in sight! The Vaporetto makes a last stop at *San Elena* before it crosses the bay to the *Lido*.

Line 82 goes down the Grand Canal more quickly than Line 1 and makes only six stops along the route from the *Ferrovia* (the Santa Lucia train station) to the *Vallaresso San Marco* landing, the last stop for Line 82, where you will be asked to disembark. Line 82 is somewhat confusing, because it begins again a bit further down the way at the *San Zaccaria* landing just past the Doge's Palace. After Line 82 starts again at the *San Zaccaria* landing, it crosses the San Marco Basin to the *San Giorgio* landing where you can get off and explore the *Chiesa e Campanile di San Giorgio Maggiore* (the Church and Bell Tower of St George Major). Line 82 then proceeds westward past drab industrial views to the *Tronchetto* (another car parking lot), then to *Piazzale Roma* (the main parking lot

Vaporetto landings along the crowded *Riva deglia Schiavoni.*

area), and after that returns to *Ferrovia* (the *Santa Lucia* train station) and then back down the Grand Canal again.

Lines 51 and 52 make a circular tour partly around Venice and then on to the *Lido*. Line 52 proceeds clockwise, while Line 51 proceeds counterclockwise. However, to make a complete circumnavigation of Venice, you will have to change boats at the *Fondamenta Nuove* landing and catch the return boat coming in the other direction from the *Lido*. The most important stops on Lines 51 and 52 to remember while using this guide are *Fondamenta Nuove* and *Ospedale*, which are alternate docks allowing you to get to the *Campo* and *Chiesa di Santi Giovanni e Paolo* (the Square and Church of Saints John and Paul), which are discussed in Tour 12 found on Track 12 of CD Two, by Vaporetto instead of trekking overland. Lines 51 and 52 also stop at *Orto*, where you can disembark to visit the wonderful church of *Madonna dell'Orto* (Madonna of the Garden). This church is filled with impressive paintings by Tintoretto, who is buried there, and is highly recommended. Lines 6, 12, and 14 will take you directly from the *San Zaccaria* landing, located in front of the famous Hotel Danieli, eastward across the San Marco Basin to the island of the *Lido*. Today, the beach resort of the *Lido*, with its gambling casinos, and high-priced cafés, does not quite live up to its reputation from its heyday in the 19th century as a prime destination for the rich and famous. Even so, if the weather is nice

Gondolas moored along the Grand Canal in the foggy winter afternoon.

and you are exhausted from walking around, the round-trip to the *Lido* and back offers an unforgettable panoramic scene on your return voyage. As you approach Venice, you will enjoy the same memorable view across the water that has inspired travelers, poets, and artists for centuries.

Line 6 goes from the *San Zaccaria* landing directly across the bay to the *Lido* and then back again. Line 14 departs from *San Zaccaria* to the *Lido*, but then runs to the islands of *Burano, Murano*, and *Torcello*. If any of the islands of *Burano, Murano*, or *Torcello* are your intended destination, you should catch Line 12 from the *Fondamenta Nuove* landing. Line 12 will take you directly to *Murano, Burano*, and then on to *Torcello*. You may wish to explore these outlying islands on your own. For the less adventurous, you can book a package tour at your hotel, at one of the Venice tourist offices, or at one of the many tables along the *Molo* and the *Riva degli Schiavoni*, where representatives of the Venetian glass factories hawk package tours. The typical tour will take you to the glass factories of *Murano*, where you will be given a glass blowing demonstration and then be offered the opportunity to buy their wares. The tour then typically proceeds to *Burano*, which is famous for its lace and colorfully painted buildings. Then the tour takes you to see the old Cathedral of *Torcello*, before returning to Venice. With a little planning, you can easily visit the islands on your own. You can explore the fishing villages and museums at your leisure and avoid the salesmen's pitches for lace and glassware.

SECTION 6

ARRIVING IN VENICE

ARRIVING IN VENICE

By Car

If you are arriving by car, you will probably be approaching Venice on the A4 *Autostrada* from the north or south. If you are traveling from the south, you will use the central *Mestre* exit. If you are coming from the north, take the *Mestre Est-Favorita* exit. To avoid high parking costs in Venice itself, you might choose to park at *Parcheggi Mestre*, the public parking deck in *Mestre*, which is next to the railroad station, before the causeway. At *Mestre* you can then catch the train to the *Ferrovia* landing or a bus to *Piazzale Roma* landing, where you can catch the Vaporetto into the city of Venice. You could also park at the *Terminal S. Giuliano*, which is nearer the water as you drive on towards Venice. There you can also catch a Vaporetto into the city.

If you're a gambler, and expense is no object, you can cross the *Ponte della Libertà* (the causeway that connects Venice with the mainland), and try to find a parking space at the *Autorimessa Comunale* (the city garage at *Piazzale Roma*) or at the *Tronchetto* (the artificial island with its own ramp leading off from the causeway before you reach the *Piazzale Roma*). Once you have parked in one of these lots, you can take a Vaporetto into the city.

If you want to avoid the risk of not finding a parking place during peak tourist times, you may wish to reserve a parking space on-line before you go. *Urbis Limen* is a new Italian on-line booking service that allows you to reserve one of the parking spaces provided at the *Piazzale Roma, Parcheggi Mestre,* or *Terminal San Giuliano*. There is no extra charge for on-line booking. Its E-mail address and Web site are listed in the guide's section "Venice Web Sites."

By Rail

Many travelers arrive at Venice at the modern *Santa Lucia* train station. It was named for the church of Santa Lucia which was demolished to make way for the railway station built by the Austrians in the late 19th century. The *Santa Lucia* station is located at the west end of the Grand Canal at the end of the causeway and links the island community with the Italian mainland. The facilities at the train station include a place for day trippers

View down the Grand Canal from the *Ferrovia* Vaporetto landing.

to leave their luggage, a money exchange, and a small tourist office with an accommodation booking service for those who arrive without hotel reservations. Be especially careful to watch your belongings in the train station, which is usually packed with hordes of travelers coming and going. Pickpockets often like to take advantage of travelers' initial confusion and excitement when they first arrive in a strange city.

Venice is well-served with direct links by train to Bologna (1 hour 35 minutes), Florence (2 hours 40 minutes), and Rome (4 hours 20 minutes). Venice is also within easy reach of Milan (2 hours 45 minutes) and the scenic towns of Padua (20 minutes) and Verona (1 hour 45 minutes). When traveling by train in Italy, remember that all train tickets must be validated before boarding by stamping the tickets in the yellow machines on the platform. If you fail to do so, you may be assessed a hefty fine when the conductor passes through the train to check tickets. You can purchase train tickets at the ticket windows or at the automated ticket machines in the station.

By Air

Venice's new Marco Polo International Airport is clean and modern. The new terminal opened in July of 2002 and has three floors. The arrivals lounge is located on the ground floor. The departure area with ticketing and baggage check-in is located on the second floor (considered as the first floor in Europe). You will also find a number of shops, cafes, and restaurants, and a 24-hour ATM on the second floor. The top floor (considered as the second floor in Europe) holds the VIP lounges, a smoking area, the chapel, and offices for the airlines and state agencies. Look over the layout of the new terminal at the airport's Web site listed in Section 7 "Venice Web Sites."

Once you exit the baggage claim area, you will come to the airport Venice Tourist Information Office (open 9:30 a.m. – 7:30 p.m.). To the left you will find the desks where you may purchase tickets for the Venice city buses, ACTV, and the intercity buses, ATVO and SITA, and the *Alilaguna* desk, where you may purchase your ticket for the boat trip to Venice by way of *Murano* and *Lido*. There are also several hotel booking offices for those arriving without hotel reservations and car rental desks.

The airport offers a circular shuttle bus service leaving every 10 minutes running between the new air terminal, the car parking lots, and the boat dock where you can catch the *Alilaguna* motorboat or a water taxi to take you into Venice.

Recorded flight information is available by telephone: Departure Information at (041) 260 9250; Arrival Information at (041) 260 9240; and General Information at (041) 260 9260. Information is also available on-line.

GETTING TO VENICE FROM MARCO POLO INTERNATIONAL AIRPORT

By Bus

It is easy to get from the airport to Venice by bus. You can take the blue ATVO intercity bus, which you can board just outside the airport. ATVO buses depart every 40 minutes. Tickets are sold by the driver or you can buy tickets at the ATVO information booth in the transportation area on the ground floor. The ATVO airport shuttle will take you directly to *Piazzale Roma*, where you can catch a Vaporetto into the city. The ACTV city bus #5 departs every 30 minutes for the 25 minute trip to *Piazzale Roma*. You must buy the ticket for the city bus in the airport at the newspaper and tobacco stand in the airport.

Once you get off either bus at *Piazzale Roma*, you will find the steps that will lead you to the Grand Canal and the Vaporetto landing on the far

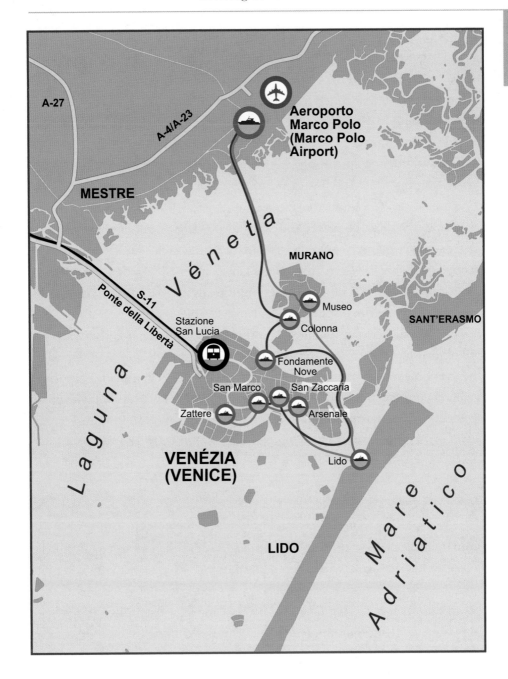

side of the bus parking lot. The landing for Line 82 is the first one you come to at the base of the stairs by the canal. The landing for Line 1 is further down on your left. Both landings are clearly marked.

By Boat

The most dramatic entrance to Venice is by boat. You can enjoy the same breathtaking view enjoyed by visitors for centuries by taking the *Alilaguna* waterbus from the Marco Polo International Airport to the *San Marco* landing in Venice, which is located near the Doge's Palace. You can buy your ticket at the *Alilaguna* desk in the ground transportation area on the ground floor of the airport. Take the shuttle to the dock, where you can board the waterbus. The first stop on the primary line *Linea Rossa* (the "Red Line") is at *Murano*, and then it goes on to the *Lido*. The waterbus then crosses the San Marco Basin and stops at the *San Marco* landing near the Doge's Palace, where you can disembark to reach St. Mark's Square. The secondary line *Linea Blu* (the "Blue Line") goes to *Murano* and then to *Fondamenta Nuove*, before proceeding directly to the *San Zaccaria* landing, where you can disembark. The trip by the primary waterbus takes about an hour and ten minutes. The trip on the Blue Line is shorter, but it is not always offered. The trip by the waterbus is only slightly longer than the combination ATVO bus and Vaporetto trip, but it provides the most exciting entry for the first-time visitor to this island city. The *Alilaguna* boat leaves hourly at ten past the hour from 6:10 a.m. until 11:10 p.m. For current fares and time schedules, you can check the *Alilaguna* Web site listed in this guide.

By Water Taxis

Venice offers a deluxe taxi service that can pick you up and whisk you from the airport dock, or from the *Santa Lucia* train station, to your hotel. Be forewarned! The sleek, wood-trimmed water taxis of Venice are unbelievably pricey. Always be sure you clearly understand the full price before you board the water taxi. There are also extra charges for each piece of luggage, plus waiting charges and nighttime surcharges. Water taxi stands are located at the dock outside the Marco Polo International Airport; outside the *Santa Lucia* train station; *Piazzale Roma; Rialto; San Marco;* and on the *Lido*.

SECTION 7

VENICE WEB SITES

A GUEST IN VENICE

This Web site provides up-to-date information about current art exhibitions, music, opera, and theater performances, films, lectures, conferences, and sports events with transportation schedules and fares, and hotels, restaurants and shops.
www.aguestinvenice.com
(English version)
www.unospitedivenezia.it
(Italian version)

VENICE.WORD

Wonderfully informative Web site updated with monthly features about local news and cultural events.
www.veniceword.com

VENICE GUIDE

Expedia.com offers a guide to the sights, with maps and current weather information on its easy-to-surf Web site.
www.expedia.com

VENEZIA NET

This Italian Web site provides information on attractions, transportation, lodging, events, and restaurants.
www.doge.it

ACTV ON LINE

The helpful and easy-to-navigate Web site for the ACTV, the Venice transportation service, is:
www.actv.it

ALILAGUNA

The Italian Web site provides fare and schedule information for the waterbus service between the Marco Polo Airport and Venice.
www.alilaguna.com

VENICE'S MARCO POLO AIRPORT

Information and maps of the airport can be found at:
www.veniceairport.it

RAIL EUROPE

Rail Europe's Web site is very user friendly and features online train schedules and allows you to book all types of European rail passes and tickets online, including rail service all over Italy.
www.raileurope.com/us/rail/fa res_schedules/index.htm

URBIS LIMEN

Reserve one of the parking spaces offered at the Venice car parking lots. There is no extra charge for on-line booking.
www.urbislimen.net/eng_preno tazione_parcheggi.php3

VENETIA

This Italian Web site offers historical anecdotes, tourism and transportation information and links to other sites.
www.venetia.it

MEETING VENICE

This Italian Web site provides a fairly up-to-date calendar of exhibitions and events and information on hotels, restaurants, and business services. **www.meetingvenice.it**

HOTELS IN VENICE

These Web sites list the names, addresses, telephone and fax numbers, and E-mail addresses of various participating hotels in Venice.
www.hoteldiscount.com
www.venicehotel.com
www.venere.it/venezia

ZOOMTA

An unconventional Italian ezine with an "alternative" viewpoint.
www.zoomata.com

ABOUT.COM - VENICE FOR VISITORS

This site provides interesting articles and annotated Web links about Venice.
www.goeurope.about.com/travel/goeurope/mmore.htm

ANCIENT GHETTO OF VENICE

These sites provide information on Venice's rich Jewish heritage.
www.doge.it/ghetto/indexi.htm
www.jewishvenice.org

CARNIVAL OF VENICE

This site provides information on Venice's most festive annual event.
www.carnivalofvenice.com

CONDÉ NAST TRAVEL'S SITE

Condé Nast Travel's Web site contains helpful articles about the city of Venice and the Veneto with its sights, restaurants, and lodgings.
www.concierge.com

VENICE CITY GUIDE

A local Web site listing Venice hotels, restaurants, events, and recommended businesses and shops.
www.elmoro.com

VENICE WEBCAM

Want to check out the weather? For a 24-hour real-time view of the Grand Canal check out:
www.turismo.regione.veneto.it/webcam/index.htm

YAHOO WEATHER SITE FOR VENICE

Yahoo provides current weather conditions and future forecasts.
weather.yahoo.com/forecast/Venice_IY_c.html

BABY BOOMER'S VENICE

This site gives interesting and practical tips for boomer travelers, with recommendations on what to see and where to stay, eat, and drink.
www.writing.org/venice.htm

ATM LOCATIONS

Use the local ATMs to obtain the best exchange rate when you buy local currency using your own bank card and personal identification number. ATM locations in Venice and world-wide can be found at:
www.mastercard.com
www.visa.com

DAILY ITALIAN NEWS

This Web site sponsored by World News will tell you what's happening in the news in Italy.
www.italy-daily.com

AZIENDA DI PROMOZIONE TURISTICA, THE APT,

The official Web site for Venice's tourist office is:
www.turismovenezia.it

CHORUS PASS

A Chorus Pass offers admission to some of Venice's most historic churches. The Chorus Web site is **www.chorus-ve.org,**

CURRENCY CONVERTER

Oanda.com offers a free "Cheat Sheet," showing the conversion rate of dollars to Euros and vice versa.
www.oanda.com/converter/ travel

VIVALDI CONCERTS AT THE CHURCH OF THE PIETA

Book your reservations on-line for music concerts at the Church of the Pieta. **www.vivaldi.it.**

GUIDE TO VENICE'S BIENNALE ART EXHIBITION

The site for information on Venice's Biennale Art Exhibition:
www.194.185.28.38/gb/index. html

VENICE'S INTERNET CAFÉ

Surf the internet, send, and check your E-mail at the "Net House" Internet Café located in Campo San Stefano. Tele. (041) 277-1190. The Café's Web site is:
www.venicepages.com

GONDOLA WEB SITE

Web site devoted to preserving the dying art of building gondolas with interesting features on gondola history and construction.
www.squero.com

SECTION 8

HISTORICAL TIMELINE

410	Visigoths capture Rome
426	Vandals sweep across Europe, invade Italy
452	Attila the Hun invades Italy; refugees flee mainland to lagoon islands
568	Lombard tribes invade Italy
590-604	Papacy of Pope Gregory the Great
632	Death of Mehmed (Mohammed)
639	Torcello Cathedral founded
	Election of the first Doge, Paoluccio Anafesta
771-814	Reign of Charlemagne; Charlemagne crowned Holy Roman Emperor by Pope; Venice defeats Pepin, son of Charlemagne
814	Construction begun of *Palazzo Ducale* (the Doge's Palace); first Venetian coins minted
828/829	Body of St. Mark stolen from Alexandria
830	Construction of first *Basilica di San Marco* (St. Mark's Basilica)
976	Reconstruction of St. Mark's Basilica after it is burned in popular uprising against Doge Pietro Candiano IV
991-1008	Reign of Doge Pietro Orseolo II; Venice establishes commercial ties with Constantinople and fights piracy
1000	Doge Pietro Orseolo II conquers pirates of the Dalmatian coast and extends Venice's control over the Adriatic Sea
1063	Third reconstruction of St. Mark's Basilica
1066	Battle of Hastings; William the Conqueror defeats Harold the Saxon
1094	St. Mark's Basilica completed; first record of the use of gondolas in Venice
1095	Pope Urban II calls for First Crusade
1099	Crusaders capture Jerusalem
1102-1108	Reign of Doge Ordelafo Falier, who orders casting of *Pala d'Oro* (Golden Altarpiece) for St. Mark's Basilica
1104	*Arsenale* founded

1172-1178	Reign of Doge Sebastiano Ziani
1173	Construction of first wooden Rialto Bridge
1177	Doge Ziani mediates "Peace of Venice" between Pope Alexander III and Frederick Barbarossa, Holy Roman Emperor
1192-1205	Reign of Doge Enrico Dandolo
1204	Crusaders sack Constantinople; Venice exacts trading concessions and returns with plunder and trophies of war, including the 4 bronze horses
1205-1229	Reign of Doge Pietro Ziani
1209	Doge Pietro Ziani orders enlargement of *Pala d'Oro;* Francis of Assisi forms order of Franciscan brotherhood
1212	Venice conquers Crete
1209	Order of Dominican brotherhood formed by Dominic of Spain
1256	Start of Hundred Years War between Venice and Genoa
1261	Byzantines recapture Constantinople
1265	Birth of author and poet Dante Alighieri (d.1321)
1268-1275	Reign of Doge Lorenzo Tiepolo
1271	Polo brothers depart for China to court of the great Kublai Khan
1289-1311	Reign of Doge Pietro Gradenigo; second war with Genoa; war with Ferrara
1295	Marco Polo returns to Venice; dictates memoirs in 1298
1307	Dante Alighieri composes *Divine Comedy*
1309	Reconstruction and extension of Doge's Palace
1310	Tiepolo Querini conspires to seize power from Great Council
1324	Death of Marco Polo
1325	Membership in Great Council made hereditary
1330	Construction begun on the *Basilica Santa Maria Gloriosa dei Frari* (Basilica of St. Mary in Glory of the Brothers) and on the Dominican *Chiesa di Santi Giovanni e Paolo* (Church of Saints John and Paul)

1343-1354	Reign of Doge Andrea Dandolo; extension of Doge's Palace; third war with Genoa
1346	Battle of Crecy; defeat of the French by England
1347-1349	First outbreak of the Black Death — the Great Plague; half of Venice's people die
1348	Boccaccio writes *Decameron*
1355	Doge Marino Falier convicted of treason and is beheaded along with artist Filippo Calendario
1378-1381	War of Chiogga with Genoa; decisive defeat of Genoese
1378-1381	Pierpaolo and Jacobello dalle Masegne sculpt statues for the iconostasis of St. Mark's Basilica
1404-1406	Venice conquers Vicenza, Verona, and Padua
1409-1410	Gentile da Fabriano paints frescos for Doge's Palace with Jacopo Bellini
1414-1423	Reign of Doge Tommaso Mocenigo; Venice extends control over entire Veneto; Priuli and Dalmatia retaken.
1415	Battle of Agincourt; Henry V defeats the French
1423-1457	Reign of Doge Francesco Foscari; Venice conquers Brescia and Bergamo; extension begun of façade of Doge's Palace (completed 1438)
1428	Birth of artist Giovanni Bellini (d. 1516)
1430-1464	Bartolomeo Bon serves as principal architect of Venice
1431	Joan of Arc burned at the stake at Rouen, France
1438	Donatello carves wooden statue of St. John the Baptist for the Florentine Chapel in the Basilica of St. Mary in Glory of the Brothers
1442	Andrea del Castagno paints frescos for the Chapel of St. Tarasius in *Chiesa di San Zaccaria* (the Church of St. Zacharias)
1443	Antonio Vivarini and Giovanni d'Alemagna complete polyptych for the Chapel of St. Tarasius in the Church of St. Zacharias; Cosimo de Medici flees Florence to monastery of *San Giorgio Maggiore* (St. George Major)
1446	Guttenberg's first printing of books

1450	Bartolomeo Bon completes sculpture over portal of *Scuola di San Marco* (School of St. Mark); Florence under rule of Medici family
1452	Ghiberti completes Gates of Paradise for Baptistery in Florence; birth of Leonardo da Vinci (d. 1519)
1453	Turks conquer Constantinople
1454	Peace of Lodi between Venice and Milan
1455-1485	War of Roses in England
1458	Construction, under Antonio Gambello, begun of the Church of St. Zacharias; Turks sack the Acropolis in Athens
1460	Construction of triumphal Gate of Arsenal by Antonio Gambello
1461	Young Leonardo da Vinci joins studio of Andrea Verrocchio
1469	Birth of Niccolo Machiavelli (d.1527); first printing press licensed in Venice
1470	Ferdinand of Aragon weds Isabella of Castile and unites Spain
1472	Gentile Bellini begins painting his series in the great hall in Doge's Palace
1473	Venice conquers Cyprus
1475	Antonio da Messina comes to Venice and popularizes use of oil paints; death of Venice's mercenary general, Bartolomeo Colleoni (b. 1400); birth of artist Michelangelo Buonarotti (d. 1564)
1477	Birth of artist Tiziano Vecellio "Titian" (d. 1576)
1479-1481	Gentile Bellini sent to Constantinople as painter to Sultan; Giovanni Bellini takes over commission for painting in Doge's Palace
1483	Mauro Codussi takes over construction of the Church of St. Zacharias; birth of artist Raffaelo Santi known as "Raphael" (d. 1520)
1486-1500	Reign of Doge Agostino Barbarigo
1488	Giovanni Bellini completes altarpiece *Madonna and Child with Saints* for sacristy of Basilica of St. Mary in Glory of the Brothers; death of Andrea del Verrocchio while casting Colleoni statue (b. 1436)
1490	Vittore Carpaccio paints the cycle *The Legend of St. Ursula*

1492	Columbus sails to America; consecration of the Basilica of St. Mary in Glory of the Brothers; birth of author Pietro Aretino (d. 1556)
1494, 1499	Invasions of Italy by France under Charles VIII; beginning of foreign domination of Italy
1495	Leonardo da Vinci begins painting *Last Supper* in Milan (completed 1498)
1496	Gentile Bellini paints *Corpus Christi Procession in St. Mark's Square*
1497	Vasco da Gama sails around Cape of Good Hope to India
1498	Michelangelo sculpts *Pieta* in Rome
1499	War begins between Venice and Turks
1501-1521	Reign of Doge Leonardo Loredan
1501	League of Cambrai formed against Venice; Michelangelo begins sculpting *David* in Florence (completed 1504)
1502	Battle of Santa Maura; Venetian force led by Jacopo Pesaro
1503	Venice signs treaty with Turks; Leonardo da Vinci paints the *Mona Lisa*
1505	Giovanni Bellini completes altarpiece *Madonna and Child* for the Church of St. Zacharias; Alessandro Leopardi completes casting statue and pedestal for Verrocchio's statue of Colleoni; Leopardi casts the three bronze flagpoles for St. Mark's Square; Dürer visits Venice; Michelangelo summoned to Rome by Pope Julius II
1507	Death of Gentile Bellini (b. 1429); Giorgione and Titian paint frescoes for *Fondaco dei Tedeschi* (trading house of the Germans)
1508	Michelangelo begins painting Sistine Chapel for Pope Julius (completed 1512); birth of architect Andrea Palladio (d. 1580)
1509	Pope Julius II joins League of Cambrai and excommunicates Venice; France joins League and declares war on Venice; 18-year old Henry VIII becomes King of England
1510	Artist Giorgione dies in outbreak of plague
1511	Pope Julius II forms Holy League with Venice and Aragon to drive French out of Italy; birth of artist Giorgio Vasari (d. 1574)
1515	Francis I conquers Milan; construction begun of *Scuola Grande di*

	San Roco (School of St. Roch) under Bartolomeo Bon, the Younger
1516	Death of Giovanni Bellini (b. 1428); Leonardo da Vinci invited to France by Francis I; Titian begins painting *Assumption of the Virgin* for Basilica of St. Mary in Glory of the Brothers (completed 1518)
1517	Martin Luther posts his 95 Theses in Wittenberg, Germany, beginning Reformation Movement
1518	Birth of artist Jacopo Robusti (Tintoretto (d. 1594)
1519	Titian begins painting *Pesaro Altarpiece* for Basilica of St. Mary in Glory of the Brothers (completed 1526); death of Emperor Maximilian I, succeeded by Charles I of Spain who becomes Holy Roman Emperor Charles V; death of Leonardo da Vinci (b. 1452); Magellan circumnavigates the globe
1520	Rule of Suleiman the Magnificent in Ottoman Empire (d. 1566); reign of Doge Andrea Gritti (d. 1538)
1526	Turks defeat Hungary in Battle of Mohacs; death of artist Vittore Carpaccio
1527	Sack of Rome by troops of Holy Roman Emperor Charles V; Jacopo Sansovino flees to Venice; Adrian Willaert becomes *maestro di capella* at St Mark's
1529	Death of Bartolomeo Bon, the Younger; Jacopo Sansovino becomes Venice's chief architect
1531	Henry VIII breaks with Roman Catholic Church
1537	Renovations by Jacopo Sansovino of St. Mark's Square, *Piazzetta*, *Loggetta*, and *Campanile*; construction begun of *Biblioteca Marciana* (Library of St. Mark), designed by Sansovino
1545	Jacopo Sansovino casts bronze sculptures for *Loggetta*
1545-1564	Council of Trent meets to discuss Reformation and begins Counter-Reformation Movement
1547	Henry VIII of England dies
1548	Tintoretto paints *St. Mark Rescuing Slave*; Titian paints *Charles V on Horseback*
1550	Giorgio Vasari writes *Lives of the Artists*

1553	Paolo Veronese paints ceiling frescoes in Doge's Palace
1556	Charles V abdicates in favor of his son, Phillip II, who becomes King of Spain and in favor of his brother, Ferdinand, who becomes Holy Roman Emperor
1558	Elizabeth I becomes Queen of England (d. 1603)
1563	Paolo Veronese paints *The Marriage at Cana*
1564	Tintoretto wins competition for painting *St. Roch In Glory* for the School of St. Roch; birth of William Shakespeare (d. 1616)
1566	Reconstruction begun under Andrea Palladio of the Church of St. George Major
1570	Turks declare war on Venice and attack Cyprus; Andrea Palladio publishes *Four Books of Architecture*
1571	Venetian commander Marcantonio Bragadin surrenders Cyprus to Turks and is tortured and killed; combined forces of Venice, the Pope, and Spain defeat Turks in pivotal naval Battle of Lepanto
1572	St. Bartholomew's Day Massacre of Hugenots in France
1573	Treaty signed between Venice and Turks; birth of artist Michelangelo da Carravaggio known as "Carravaggio" (d. 1610); Paolo Veronese summoned before Inquisition for his painting of the *Last Supper*
1574	Doge's Palace damaged by fire
1575-1576	Outbreak of plague kills one third of Venice's population
1576	Construction begins under Andrea Palladio of *Il Redentore* (the Church of the Redeemer); death of Titian in the great plague; Alessandro Vittoria sculpts *St. Jerome* for Basilica of St. Mary in Glory of the Brothers
1577	Doge's Palace largely destroyed by fire; reconstruction begun
1582	Venetian Constitution amended with limitations imposed on the power of Council of Ten
1585	Paolo Veronese paints *Apotheosis of Venice* in newly rebuilt great hall in Doge's Palace
1588	Defeat of Spanish Armada by England; death of artist, Veronese; construction begun of Rialto Bridge designed by Antonio da Ponte

1589	Construction of the *Prigioni Nuove* (the New Prisons) next to Doge's Palace
1591	Construction of Rialto Bridge completed
1595	Tintoretto dies (b. 1518)
1599	Construction of *Ponte dei Sospiri* (Bridge of Sighs) by Antonio Contino; construction of Globe Theater in London by Richard Burbage
1606-1612	Reign of Doge Leonardo Dona
1609	Galileo demonstrates his new invention, the telescope, to Doge Leonardo Dona from the top of the *Campanile*
1613	Monteverdi appointed choirmaster of St. Mark's Basilica
1615	Galileo summoned before Inquisition
1616	War between Venice and Austria; death of Shakespeare (b. 1564)
1630	Election of Doge Nicolo Contarini; devastating plague breaks out in Venice; Puritans found Boston
1631	Construction begun of the *Chiesa di Santa Maria della Salute* (the Church of St. Mary of Health) designed by Baldassare Longhena
1645	Turkish Venetian War begins over control of Crete 1669
1669	Venice loses Crete to Ottoman Turks; Justin Le Court carves sculpture group for altar of the Church of St. Mary of Health
1678	Earthquake rocks Venice; birth of composer Antonio Vivaldi (d. 1741)
1685	Birth of German composers, Johan Sebastian Bach (d. 1750) and George Frederick Handel (d. 1757)
1687	Consecration of Church of St. Mary of Health; Venetian forces led by Francesco Morosini attack Turks in Athens; Parthenon at Acropolis severely damaged by Venetian bombardment
1697	Birth of artist Giovanni Antonio Canal known as "Canaletto" (d. 1768)
1703	Antonio Vivaldi becomes concertmaster of *Chiesa di Santa Maria della Visitazione* (the Church of the Pieta)
1718	Venice surrenders Greek Islands of the Peloponnese (Morea) to Turks; end of Venetian Empire

1720	Café Florian opens in St. Mark's Square
1725	Birth of Venetian adventurer and writer Giovanni Giacomo Casanova (d. 1798)
1756	Birth of German composer Wolfgang Amadeus Mozart (d. 1791); Casanova escapes from prison in Venice; flees Inquisition to France
1757	Birth of sculptor Antonio Canova (d. 1822)
1768	Death of artist Canaletto
1769	Birth of Napoleon, future emperor (d. 1821)
1770	Death of artist Giovanni Tiepolo (b. 1696)
1775	Café Quadri opens in St. Mark's Square
1786	Mozart's *Marriage of Figaro* premiers in Vienna
1789	Storming of the Bastille in Paris
1796	Napoleon establishes Lombard Republic in Northern Italy
1797	Napoleon seizes Mantua; proclaims end of Venetian Republic; Doge Lodovico Manin deposed; Great Council dissolved; Treaty of Campo Formio ends war between France and Austria; treaty briefly transfers control of Venice to Austria
1798	Napoleon captures Rome; proclaims Roman Republic
1804	Napoleon becomes Emperor of France
1805	Napoleon crowned King of Italy; Treaty of Pressburg transfers control of Venice to Kingdom of Italy
1806	Napoleon orders suppression of Venice's *scuole* and guilds; closes many churches and monasteries
1807	*Chiesa di San Geminiano* (church of St. Geminiano) demolished to create *Ala Napoleonica* (Napoleonic wing of Palace)
1814	Napoleon abdicates and exiled to Elba; control of Venice transferred to Austria
1821	Death of Napoleon at Elba
1822	Death of sculptor Antonio Canova
1836	Construction of *Palazzo Patriarcale* (Palace of the Patriarch)

1841	Construction begins of railway causeway from Mestre to Venice, linking Venice to mainland (completed 1846)
1848-1849	Venice revolts against Austria; Daniele Manin proclaimed president of new Republic of Venice; Austria counterattacks; Venice bombarded by Austria; Venice suffers outbreak of cholera and surrenders; Daniele Manin flees to Paris
1853	Monument to Titian erected by Hapsburg King in Basilica of St. Mary in Glory of the Brothers; John Ruskin publishes *Stones of Venice*
1859	Second War of Independence against Austria led by Piedmont, with France as ally
1860	Garibaldi and his 1,000 Red Shirts declare Victor Emmanuel II King of Italy; invasion of Papal States by Victor Emmanuel; election of Abraham Lincoln as 16th U.S. President; South Carolina secedes from Union
1861	Naples surrenders to Garibaldi; Italy proclaimed a united kingdom with Victor Emmanuel II as King and Turin as its capitol
1863	Lincoln issues Emancipation Proclamation; Battle of Gettysburg
1865	Florence becomes capital of Kingdom of Italy
1866	Venice votes to join Kingdom of Italy; American Civil War ends
1869	Opening of Suez Canal
1870	Rome declared capital of Kingdom of Italy
1883	Death of Richard Wagner in Venice (b. 1813)
1889	Gilbert and Sullivan's *The Gondoliers* premiers in London
1895	First *Biennale* Art Exhibition held in Venice
1902	*Campanile* suddenly collapses in St. Mark's Square
1903	Patriarch Sarto of Venice elected Pope Pius X
1912	Thomas Mann writes *Death in Venice;* rebuilt *Campanile* is dedicated
1914	Assassination of Archduke Francis Ferdinand, heir to Austrian throne; First World War begins; Italy joins the Allies
1918	Armistice ends WWI

1922-1926	The "March on Rome"; Mussolini becomes prime minister then proclaimed *Duce* (leader)
1926	Mestre granted township status
1933	Adolph Hitler elected German Chancellor; Franklin Roosevelt elected 32nd U.S. President
1931	Causeway completed, linking Venice to mainland traffic
1932	First Venice Film Festival held in Venice
1934	Hitler and Mussolini meet in Venice
1939-1945	WWII
1945	Execution of Mussolini
1946	Abdication of Victor Emmanuel III and accession of King Umberto II; proclamation of Italian Republic
1959	Patriarch Roncalli of Venice elected Pope John XXIII
1960	Venice Marco Polo airport opens
1966	Terrible floods devastate Venice and Florence
1970	Luchino Visconti films *Death in Venice*
1978	Patriarch Luciani of Venice elected Pope John Paul I, but dies 33 days later
1979	Death of Peggy Guggenheim; Venice's Celebration of *Carnivale* is revived

SECTION 9

GLOSSARY

Aisle Side of church on either side of nave, usually divided by columns or arches

Albergo Small room used for meetings, usually on the upper floors of a *scuola*

Allegory (Grk. *allegoria* - to picture differently) Depiction of abstract concepts or ideas by human figures or scenes

Apostle (Grk. *apostolos* - messenger) The name given to Christ's original twelve disciples and Paul, who were chosen by Jesus to carry on his teaching

Apse Semi-circular domed ceiling at the east end of church, usually above the high altar

Annunciation (Lat. *annuciare* - to announce) Frequent subject of religious paintings. According to Gospel of Luke 1:26-38, Archangel Gabriel appeared to Mary to announce that she would bear a son and that he would be called Jesus

Arcade Arch or row of arches supported by columns

Arch Load-bearing, vaulted opening in wall, which is supported by pillars or columns

Architrave Main beam supported by columns and bearing the weight of the structure

Atrium Forecourt of church, usually enclosed with arcade also known as vestibule

Baldachin Canopy of bronze or stone, usually over the altar, throne, or catafalque and supported by columns.

Balustrade Railing (with vase-like balusters) along edge of balcony, terrace, bridge, staircase, or eaves of building

Baroque Style of art from the late 16th century to mid 18th century. Usually emphasizes spectacle or theatrical elements; associated with the Roman Catholic Counter-Reformation use of art to re-energize the faithful

Basilica	Large, rectangular building, usually with nave and two or four side aisles; adopted by early Byzantine church from the Roman style for public buildings and later used in religious structures
Bas relief	Sculpture that projects only slightly from its background; low relief
Biennale	(Itl. - every two years)
Bozzeto	(Itl. - sketch or small preparatory model)
Bucintoro	Galley used by Doge for ceremonial occasions
Byzantine art	Art of the Byzantium (the Eastern Roman Empire) with its capital Constantinople (today's Istanbul from 324AD) until conquered by the Turks in 1453; typified by rigid, stylized, iconic figures
Calle	(Itl. - narrow street) Term used in Venice for narrow street that is open at both ends
Camera	(Itl. - room)
Campanile	(from Itl. *campana* - bell) Bell Tower, usually freestanding
Campo	(Itl. - field) All squares in Venice are called "*Campi*" (fields) except *Piazza San Marco* (St. Mark's Square)
Capital	Head of column or pillar
Cartoon	Preparatory drawing
Chapel	Small room in church used for special purpose
Chiaroscuro	(Itl. – light and shade) Art term for contrasting use of light and dark in painting
Chiesa	(Itl. – church)
Choir Screen	Screen or wall-like division between the choir and clergy and the laity, often painted or carved (also known as the Rood Screen or Iconostasis); abolished in Western Churches by Council of Trent (1545-63)
Cenacolo	(Itl. - Last Supper) Frequent subject of religious art

Chancel   Enclosed space around the altar; originally reserved for clergy and choir

Cloister   Quadrangle, with covered walkways and central garden adjacent to churches or monastery used as a place for prayer and reflection

Condottieri   Mercenary generals, or warriors for hire; used by Italian city states in 14th and 15th centuries to lead mercenary armies

Cornu   Doge's ceremonial hat, horned and made of red velvet

Crenellations   Battlements

Cupola   (Itl. - Dome)

Diptych   Painting in two sections or panels, usually hinged

Doge   (Derived from Latin *Dux* – leader) Elected Venetian head of state

Duomo   (Itl. - cathedral) Official seat of the Bishop, usually city's principal church

Façade   Architectural face, decorative treatment of front of building

Fondamenta   Term used in Venice to describe a broad street along a canal

Fresco   Painting made on wet plaster surface

Frieze   Decorative band on buildings

Gesso   Base made of chalk or gypsum; used in preparing a panel or canvas as a base for painting

Gilding   Application of gold leaf

Glaze   Application of thin layers of transparent paint to modify tone or give effect

Gothic   (Derived from Itl. *gotico* – barbaric) Originally a derogatory term used to describe artistic style of

	Middle Ages—from 12th century until early 16th century; features pointed arches, ribbed arches, and carved decorations with emphasis on verticality and use of external buttresses; Gothic sculpture utilizes elongated stylized forms
Greek Cross	Religious construction of building with nave and transept of equal length, as contrasted with the traditional Latin cross construction, where the cross arms of the transept are shorter than the nave
Guilds	Associations of trades, artists or craftsmen; superceded by the *scuoli* - lay brotherhoods or confraternities in Venice
High Renaissance	High point of the Renaissance period of art (c.1490-1520) typified by Michelangelo, Raphael, Leonardo in the south and Titian in Venice.
Icon	(Grk. - Portrait) Painting on panel depicting two-dimensional stylized forms, often with likeness of the Virgin Mary, Jesus, or saints; usually in traditional Byzantine style
Iconostasis	Wall dividing sanctuary from church hall or chancel; often decorated with icons in Orthodox tradition
Impasto	(Itl. – mixture) Painting technique, where paint is applied thickly to canvas or panel, sometimes with palette or artist's fingers
Lantern	Circular structure on top of dome, usually with windows or arches
Latin Cross	Religious construction of building with vertical arm of the nave longer than the horizontal cross arm of the transept
Loggia	(Itl. - balcony or gallery)
Lunette	Semi-circular frame, in ceiling of vault, holding painting or sculpture

Maesta (Itl. – majesty or grandeur) Altarpiece depicting enthroned Madonna and Child, usually surrounded by saints and angels

Mannerism style associated with the period between High Renaissance and Baroque (c. 1520-1620); by virtuosity and breaking rules of convention; elongated figures and turbulent action typified by Tintoretto

Molo (Itl. - canal side promenade, wharf, jetty, or quay)

Mosaic Ornamental decoration, from Byzantine tradition, using multicolored stones or glass to ornament walls or floors

Museo (Itl. – museum)

Narthex Anteroom of a church; vestibule leading to the nave (interior) of a church

Nave Central body (interior) of a church

Niche Recess in wall, usually for statue or decorative figures

Oil painting Paint with pigment mixed in oil, usually linseed oil; believed to have been introduced to Venice by Antonio de Messina, but popularized and advanced by the Bellini family workshop

Obelisk Stone, ornamental column usually tapering at top

Opera Office in charge of Cathedral's structure

Pala Altarpiece

Palazzo (Itl. - palace or mansion)

Passion Depiction of the suffering of Christ between the Last Supper and Crucifixion

Pediment Triangular area below roof of building, and over doors and windows, often with decorative sculpture

Piazza (Itl. - square or market place) In Venice only St. Mark's Square is called a piazza; all the other squares are called *campi* (fields)

136

Pieta	(Itl. – pity, compassion, or mercy) In art, a traditional painting of the Virgin Mary mourning the crucified Christ
Pigment	Coloring matter, mixed with binding agent to become paint
Perspective	System of depicting three-dimensional figures on two-dimensional surfaces
Polyptych	Painting made on more than three sections or panels
Ponte	(Itl. – bridge)
Porphyry	(Grk *porphyros* - purple). The term originally applied to Egyptian rock composed of crystals embedded in a red or purple medium.
Predella	(Itl. – altar-step) Painting(s) located below an altarpiece, usually smaller, and related to the subject of the altarpiece
Putto (putti)	(Itl. - small child) Decorative nude figure of child or baby in Renaissance and Baroque art, often with wings; sometimes called a cherub or related to Cupid figure
Quatrefoil	Four-lobed design of Gothic art and window framing
Quattrocento	(Itl. - four hundred) Term often used to describe the 15th century Italian age
Refectory	Dining hall in monastery
Relic	Corpse or portion of body of revered saint
Reliquary	A vessel created to hold the relics of a saint
Renaissance	(Fr. – rebirth; Itl. – *rinascimento*) movement in the 14th to 16th centuries; term used by Giorgio Vasari in 1550; tradition term for the rebirth or revival of classical art, architecture, and literature under the influence of classical Greek and Roman models; typified by emphasis on man and humanism, rather than being focused on the church and Christian doctrine

Rio   (Itl. – brook, stream) Venetian for canal

Riva   (Itl. – bank, shore) Term used in Venice for narrow passageway along a canal

Risorgimento   (Itl. - resurgence) Term used to describe the mid-19th century movement reviving Italian nationalism

Rococo   (Fr. - *rocaille* - rock-work) (c. 1715—1750s) Elegant and ornate art style following Baroque Period, with emphasis on lightness and decorative curves; frequent use of scallop shell motif; seen as reaction to "heaviness" of late Baroque era

Romanesque   Western style of 11th and 12th centuries, typified by rounded arches and massive pillars; derived from antique Roman style

Ruga   (Itl. – wrinkle) Term used in Venice for "street"

Sacristy   Room in church for priests to dress and prepare for service, and where liturgical objects are kept

Salizzada   Term used in Venice for "wide street"

Sestiere   Term used in Venice for "district"

Sfumato   (Derived from Itl. - *sfumare* - to tone down, shade, or end in smoke) Art technique of creating smoky effect blending light to dark

Scuola   (Itl. – school) Venetian lay brotherhood or charitable confraternity, usually devoted to religious or social concerns; derived from medieval penitent or apprentice fraternities, usually made up of same ethnic or trade group; Venice recognized six major *Scuole* and numerous smaller *scuole*

Sottoportego   (Itl. – entrance under a building leading to courtyard or *campo*)

Tempera	Paint technique where pigment was mixed with egg yolk as the bonding medium; associated with painting in the 12th to 15th centuries
Tessere	(Itl. – to weave) Small cubes of colored glass or stone used in mosaics
Tondo	(Itl. – plate or saucer) Art term for circular painting or sculpture in relief; popular in 15th century
Traghetto	(Itl. – ferry)
Transept	The cross arm of a church plan; the shorter, horizontal arm in Latin Cross church plan
Travertine	Limestone building material
Trefoil	Gothic decorative pattern using three identical clover leaves; three-lobed ornamentation, usually in windows; ornament or symbol in the form of a stylized threefold leaf
Triptych	Painting in three sections or panels, usually hinged, with central panel most prominent and sometimes painted on both sides
Trompe l'oeil	Art designed to "trick the eye"
Vaporetto	(Itl. - little steamboat) Venetian waterbus
Volute	A spiral or scroll-shaped ornamental detail used as a buttress to support a dome

SECTION 10

ATTRACTION ADMISSION FEES AND OPENING TIMES

The admission fees to museums and churches constantly change. Even with the latest information, the moment a guidebook goes to press, the prices often become outdated. The change from the Lira to the Euro has further complicated providing accurate information. The opening and closing times generally change with longer hours of operation in the summer months and earlier closing times in winter. They may frequently vary without notice due to staff shortages. Current information on opening and closing times and admission fees can be found at one of the recommended Venice Web sites listed in this guide such as www.aguestinvenice.com. The city of Venice currently offers two types of combination admission tickets to various municipal museums.

Museum Card

The Museum Card allows entry to the *Musei di Piazza San Marco* (the Museums of St. Mark's Square), which are the Doge's Palace, the Correr Museum, the Archeological Museum, and the Monuments Hall of the Library of St. Mark. You cannot buy separate tickets to these sites. The Museum Card costs €9,50 and admission is valid for 3 months.

Museum Pass

The Museum Pass allows entry to the Museums of St. Mark's Square, plus it includes admission to the Museums of 18th Century Culture, which are the *Ca' Rezzonico, Casa Goldoni,* and *Palazzo Mocenigo.* The Museum Pass is also good for admission to the museums on the islands of *Burano, Murano,* and *Torcello.* You may choose to buy separate admission tickets to *Ca' Rezzonico, Casa Goldoni, Palazzo Mocenigo,* and the island Museums. The Museum Pass costs €15,50 and admission is valid for 3 months.

Tour 1
Palazzo Ducale **(Doge's Palace)**
Piazzetta San Marco (entrance through the doorway on waterfront or through Porta della Carta) ꝏ Vaporetto Lines 1, 52, *San Marco* landing
Admission €9,50 (Museum Card); Open Monday - Sunday 9:00 a.m. - 7:00 p.m. (April 1 until October 31); 9:00 a.m. - 5:00 p.m. (November 1 until March 31)

Museo Civico Correr (Correr Museum)

St. Mark's Square (entrance through Napoleonic Wing, west side of
St. Mark's Square), Admission €9,50 (Museum Card);
Open daily 9:00 a.m. - 7:00 p.m. (April 1 until October 31) and
9:00 a.m. - 5:00 p.m. (November 1 until March 31)

Sale Monumentali della Biblioteca Nazionale Marciana (Monumental Hall of the Library of St. Mark)

St. Mark's Square, Admission €9,50 (Museum Card) Admission through the
Correr Museum. Open daily from 9:00 a.m. - 7:00 p.m. (April 1 until
October 31) and 9:00 a.m. - 5:00 p.m. (November 1 until March 31)

Museo Archeologico (Archeological Museum)

St. Mark's Square, Admission €9,50 (Museum Card) Admission through the
Correr Museum. Open daily from 9:00 a.m. - 7:00 p.m. (April 1 until
October 31) and 9:00 a.m. - 5:00 p.m. (November 1 until March 31)

Tour 2
Basilica di San Marco (St. Mark's Basilica)

St. Mark's Square ➻ Vaporetto Lines 1, 52, 82, San Marco landing
Admission free; Open Monday - Saturday 9:30 a.m. - 5:00 p.m.,
Sunday 1:30 p.m. - 5:00 p.m.

Pala d'Oro (Golden Altarpiece)

Admission €1,55; Open weekdays 9:45 a.m. - 4:30 p.m., weekends and
holy days 2:00 p.m. - 4:30 p.m.

Tesoro di San Marco (Treasury of St. Mark)

Admission €2,70; Open weekdays 9:45 a.m. - 4:30 p.m., weekends and
holy days 2:00 p.m. - 4:30 p.m.

Museo Marciano (Museum of St. Mark) Loggia dei Cavalli (Gallery of the Horses)

Admission €1,55; Open Monday - Friday 9:45 a.m. - 5:00 p.m.

Tour 3 and 4
Campanile di San Marco (Bell Tower of St. Mark)

St. Mark's Square ↪ Vaporetto Lines 1, 52, 82, *San Marco* landing
Admission €6,00; Open daily 9:00 a.m. – 7:00 p.m.

Tour 5
Chiesa San Zaccaria (Church of St. Zacharias)

Castello, Campo San Zaccaria ↪ Vaporetto Lines 1, 52, 82, *S. Zaccaria* landing
Admission to church is free; admission to St. Tarasius' Chapel €2,70; Open daily 10:00 a.m. – 12:00 a.m., 4:00 p.m. – 6:00 p.m.

Tour 6
Scuola Dalmatia di S. Giorgio degli Schiavoni (School of St. George of the Dalmatians)

Castello, Ponte dei Greci ↪ Vaporetto Line 1, 52, *S. Zaccaria* landing
Admission €2,58; Open Tuesday - Saturday 10:00 a.m. - 12:00 p.m., 3:30 p.m. - 6:30 p.m., Sunday 10:00 a.m. - 12:30 p.m.

Tour 7
Chiesa e Campanile di San Giorgio Maggiore (Church of St. George Major and Bell Tower)

Island of S. Giorgio ↪ Vaporetto Line 82, *S. Giorgio* landing
Admission free; Open daily 9:30 a.m. - 12:30 p.m., 2:30 p.m. - 6:00 p.m.; Admission to Bell Tower €3,00.

Tour 8
Basilica Santa Maria Gloriosa dei Frari (Basilica of St. Mary in Glory of the Brothers)

San Polo, Campo di Frari ↪ Vaporetto Lines 1, 82, S. *Toma* landing
Admission €2,00 or Chorus Pass €8,00; Open weekdays 9:00 a.m. - 6:00 p.m., Sundays and holy days 1:00 p.m. - 6:00 p.m.

Tour 11

Chiesa di Santa Maria della Salute (Church of St. Mary of Health)

Dorsoduro, punta de la Dogana ∽ Vaporetto Line 1, *Salute* landing
Admission free; Open Monday - Sunday 9:00 a.m. – 12:00 p.m.,
3:00 p.m. - 5:30 p.m.

Tour 12

Chiesa dei Santi Giovanni e Paolo Zanipolo (Church of Sts. John and Paul)

Campo Santi Giovanni e Paolo ∽ Vaporetto Line 52, *Ospedale Civile* or
Fondamenta Nuove landings
Admission free; Open Monday - Saturday 7:30 a.m. - 12:30 p.m.,
3:00 p.m. - 7:00 p.m.; Sunday 3:00 p.m. - 6:00 p.m.

OTHER RECOMMENDED SITES OF INTEREST

Gallerie dell' Accademia (Academy Museum)

Dorsoduro, Campo della Carità ∽ Vaporetto Lines 1, 82, *Accademia* landing
Admission €6,50; Open Monday 9:00 a.m. - 2:00 p.m., Tuesday - Sunday
8:15 a.m. - 7:15 p.m. Offers a combined admission ticket €9,50 to *Ca'
d'Oro* / Franchetti Gallery and Oriental Museum.

Ca' d'Oro (House of Gold) Galleria Franchetti (Franchetti Gallery)

Cannaregio, Ca'd'Oro ∽ Vaporetto Line 1, *Ca' d'Oro* landing
Admission €2,00 or on combined ticket with Academy and Oriental
Museums €9,50; Open daily 9:00 a.m. - 2:00 p.m.

Collezione Peggy Guggenheim (Guggenheim Collection)

Dorsoduro, Palazzo Venier dei Leoni ∽ Vaporetto Line 1, *Salute* landing.
Admission €8,00; Open Wednesday - Monday 10:00 a.m. - 6:00 p.m.

Museo Storico Navale (Museum of Naval History)

Castello, Campo San Biagio ∽ Vaporetto Line 1, *Arsenale* landing
Admission €1,55; Open Monday - Saturday 8:45 a.m. - 1:30 p.m.

Ca' Rezzonico/ Museo del Settecento Veneziano (Museum of the Venetian 18th Century)

Dorsoduro, Fondamenta Rezzonico ∽ Vaporetto Line 1, *Rezzonico* landing
Admission €9,50 (Museum Card) or separate admission €6,71;
Open Wednesday - Monday 10:00 a.m. - 5:00 p.m.

Scuola Grande di San Roco (School of St. Roch)

San Polo, Salizzada San Rocco Frari ∽ Vaporetto Line 1, *S. Toma* landing
Admission €5,16; Open from March 28 to November 2, 9:00 a.m. - 5.30
p.m. on all days; open from November to February, Monday to Friday
10:00 a.m. - 1:00 p.m., and Saturday and Sunday 10:00 a.m. - 4:00 p.m.;
open during Christmas week and Carnival week 10:00 a.m. - 4:00 p.m.

Museo d' Arte Orientale (Museum of Oriental Art)

Santa Croce, Ca' Pesaro ∽ Vaporetto Line 1, *S. Stae* landing
Admission €2,00 or combined ticket with Academy and Ca' d'Oro /
Franchetti Gallery €9,50; Open Tuesday – Sunday 9:00 a.m.-2:00 p.m.

Casa Goldoni (House of Goldoni)

San Polo ∽ Vaporetto Lines 1, 82, S. *Toma* landing
Admission €9,50 (Museum Card) or separate admission, €4,13; Open
10:00 a.m. - 4:00 p.m.; closed Sunday.

Museo di Palazzo Mocenigo (Mocenigo Palace Center for the Study of the History of Fabrics and Costumes)

Santa Croce, Salizzada S. Stae ∽ Vaporetto Line 1, *S. Stae*, landing
Admission €4,13; Palace: Open 10:00 a.m. - 5:00 p.m.; Tuesday - Friday
(closed Saturday, Sunday, Monday), Library: Tuesday - Thursday 10:00
a.m. - 1:30 p.m., Wednesday - Friday. 8.30 a.m. - 1.30 p.m.

Museo Comunitá Ebracia (Museum of the Jewish Community)

Cannaregio, Campo del Ghetto Nuovo ∽ Vaporetto Lines 1, 82,
S. Marcuola landing
Admission €8,00; Open Sunday – Friday. closed Saturday and Jewish
holidays, 10:00 a.m. – 5:30 p.m.

Museo Diocesano di Arte Sacra (Museum of Sacred Art)
Castello, ponte de la Canonica convento di S.Apollonia
Admission free (donations accepted); Open: Monday - Saturday 10.30
a.m.-12.30 p.m.

Museo Querini Stampalia (Museum of the Querini Stampalia family)
Castello, Campo S. Maria Formosa ↝ Vaporetto Lines 1, 52, S. Zaccaria
landing
Admission €6,00; Open Tuesday - Thursday, Sunday 10:00 a.m. – 6:00 p.m.,
Friday and Saturday 10:00 a.m. to 10:00 p.m.

CHORUS PASS

The Churches of Venice Association and the Venice tourist office offers a Chorus Pass that provides entry to the *Basilica Santa Maria Gloriosa dei Frari* (Basilica of St. Mary in Glory of the Brothers) and fourteen of Venice's less frequently visited churches. The Chorus Pass is also sold in each of the churches covered in the program. The Chorus Pass is good for one year. For an extra fee, audio tapes with detailed narratives are available at the churches visited on the Chorus Pass.

The churches included on the pass are the *Basilica Santa Maria Gloriosa dei Frari* (Basilica of St. Mary in Glory of the Brothers), *Chiesa di Santa Maria del Giglio* (Church of St. Mary of the Lilies), *Chiesa di S. Stefano* (Church of St. Stephen), *Chiesa di Santa Maria Formosa* (Church of St. Mary of Formosa), *Chiesa di Santa Maria dei Miracoli* (Church of the Miraculous Mary), *Chiesa di S. Polo* (Church of St. Paul), *Chiesa di S. Giacomo dall'Orio* (Church of St. James dall'Orio), *Chiesa di S. Stae* (Church of St. Stae), *Chiesa di S. Alvise* (Church of St. Alvise), *Chiesa di Madonna dell'Orto* (Church of the Madonna of the Garden), *Chiesa di S. Pietro di Castello* (Church of St. Peter in Castello), *Chiesa Il Redentore* (Church of the Redeemer), *Chiesa di S. Sebastiano* (Church of St. Sebastian), *Chiesa di Gesuati* (Church of the Gesuati) and *Chiesa di San Giovanni Elemosinario* (Church of St. John). The Churches are open Monday through Saturday from 10:00 a.m. - 5:00 p.m.; Sunday 1:00 p.m. - 5:00 p.m./ Basilica of St. Mary in Glory of the Brothers is open Monday - Saturday, 9:00 a.m. - 6:00 p.m.; Sunday 1:00 p.m. - 6:00 p.m. Chorus Pass €8,00, admission to single church, €2,00.

REFERENCE AND FURTHER READING

Andreolo, Aldo, and Elisabetta Borsetti, Michael Gluckstein (Translator): *Venice Remembers,* Publisher: Editrice; ISBN 88-900457-0-1; 1st edition (1999)

Boulton, Susie, and Deni Brown: *Eyewitness Travel Guide to Venice and the Veneto,* Publisher: DK Publishing; ISBN: 1564588610; 1st edition (January 1, 1997)

Fodors (Editor): *Fodor's Citypack Venice,* Publisher: Fodors Travel Pubns; ISBN: 0676901735; 3rd Bk & map edition (March 5, 2002)

Fortini Brown, Patricia: *Art and Life in Renaissance Venice,* Publisher: Harry N. Abrams; ISBN: 0810927470; (September 1997)

Fortini Brown, Patricia: *Venice & Antiquity: The Venetian Sense of the Past,* Publisher: Yale Univ Pr; ISBN: 0300067003; (March 1997)

Garrett, Martin: *A Cultural and Literary Companion* (Cities of the Imagination Series), Publisher: Interlink Pub Group; ISBN:1566563690; (April 2001)

Hartt, Frederick, and David G. Wilkins (Editor): *History of Italian Renaissance Art: Painting, Sculpture, Architecture,* Publisher: Lund Humphries; International Fund for Monuments; ASIN: 0853314365; 3rd revised ed. (1998)

Honour, Hugh: *The Companion Guide to Venice* (Companion Guides), Publisher: Boydell & Brewer; ISBN: 1900639246; 4th edition (July 1998)

Kahn, Robert (Editor): *City Secrets: Florence, Venice, and the Towns of Italy,* Publisher: Little Bookroom; ISBN: 1892145014; (June 9, 2001)

Kaminski, Marion: *Venice: Art & Architecture,* Publisher: Konemann; ISBN: 3829026676; (August 2000)

Links, J.G.: *Venice for Pleasure,* Publisher: Pallas Athene Pub; ISBN: 1873429401; 7th Rev. edition (April 2001)

Lombardi, Matt (Editor), and David Cashion (Editor): *Fodor's Venice and the Veneto,* Publisher: Fodors Travel Pubns; ISBN: 0676902138; 2nd edition (March 5, 2002)

MacAdam, Alta: *Blue Guide Venice,* Publisher: W.W. Norton & Company; ISBN: 0393322483; 7th edition (December 2001)

Norwich, John Julius (Editor): *Traveller's Companion to Venice (The Traveller's Companion Series),* Publisher: Interlink Pub Group; ISBN: 1566564654; (August 2002)

Norwich, John Julius: *A History of Venice,* Publisher: Vintage Books; ISBN: 0679721975; (June 1989)

Rabb, Theodore K.: *Renaissance Lives: Portraits of an Age,* Publisher: Basic Books; ISBN: 0465068006; (January 1, 2001)

Romanelli, Giandomenco (Editor), Janet Angelini and Elizabeth Clegg (Translators): *Venice: Art & Architecture,* Publisher: Konemann; ISBN: 3895085936; Slipcase edition (June 1999)

Simonis, Damien: *Lonely Planet Venice,* Publisher: Lonely Planet; ISBN: 1864503211; 2nd edition (May 2002)

Steves, Rick: *Italy 2003,* Publisher: Avalon Travel Publishing; ISBN: 1566914647; (December 2002)

Steves, Rick: *Venice 2003,* Publisher: Avalon Travel Publishing; ISBN: 1566914833; (December 2002)

Vio, Ettore (Editor), Huw Evans (Translator): *The Basilica of St. Mark in Venice,* Publisher: Riverside Book Company; ASIN: 1878351559; 1st edition (April 2000)

Wills, Garry: *Venice: Lion City,* Publisher: Simon & Schuster; ISBN: 0684871904; (September 2001)

Zuffi, Stefano: *Art in Venice,* Publisher: Abradale Press; ISBN: 0810981734; (April 2002)

ACKNOWLEDGEMENTS

I am grateful to the charming pair of elderly English women I met several years ago while touring the island of Torcello near Venice. They had taken a tour offered by a local agency that morning. They told me how their wonderful tour guide was so knowledgeable and interesting that she brought the history of Venice to life for them. These were very well-traveled women and so I took the suggested tour the following day, but ended up with a different tour guide who was less than inspiring. From that disappointment, the idea for this series was born.

Deep gratitude is owed to my friends Mark Bishop, Steve and Mary McCall Cash, Mark Wasley, Tedi and Joel Godard, Rebecca Landers, Jan Bolgla, and Chuck Rice for their review of endless drafts and for their helpful suggestions. Without their patient advice and input this book would not have been possible. I am also indebted to my college history professor, Dr. Joseph Berrigan, now Professor Emeritus of the History Department of the University of Georgia, who taught me that history is more than the dates of battles and the names of rulers, but is the story of the lives of real people and the development and interplay of their ideas as reflected in their art, literature, architecture, and music. The seeds planted in those engaging and inspired lectures bloomed into a lifelong love of history and a boundless enthusiasm for European travel that has enriched my life beyond measure.

ABOUT THE NARRATOR

Venice In Context is narrated by Joel Godard, a veteran New York actor, spokesman, and Voice/Over talent. He has worked in TV, film, and radio for many years and has done on-camera and Voice/Over work in numerous commercials. He worked as an NBC network staff announcer before becoming the announcer for *Dateline NBC* with Jane Pauley and Stone Phillips. He has been heard as the network announcer for recent NBC broadcasts of Macy's Thanksgiving Day Parade and the lighting of the great Christmas tree at Rockefeller Center. Currently, he is the announcer for the *Late Night with Conan O'Brien*, where he frequently makes on-camera appearances in the show's comedy sketches.

ABOUT THE AUTHOR

Venice In Context is the first in a series of guides for the independent traveler, *Europe In Context,* conceived and written by Robert S. Wayne and published by Independent International Travel, LLC. Author Robert S. Wayne is a graduate of the University of Georgia where he obtained a degree in Vocal Music Performance and later went on to earn a law degree. He is the former Managing Editor of the Georgia Journal of International and Comparative Law. The author spent two summers studying opera at the American Institute for Musical Studies in Graz, Austria. He is now an attorney living in Atlanta, Georgia, where he balances the demands of a busy practice with extensive travel and writing. The project *Europe In Context* reflects his life-long passion for music, history, and art and his experiences in over twenty years of traveling independently and exploring the treasures of Europe.

INDEX

Index

Index

ABOUT ORDERING

ORDERING ON LINE

Consumers can buy on-line with confidence directly from our secure Web site at: **europeincontext.com**

ORDERING BY PHONE

Call our toll-free number 1-800-247-6553

ORDERING BY MAIL OR FAX

Fax orders for purchase by credit card to (419) 281-6883 or send your check by mail to:

**INDEPENDENT
INTERNATIONAL TRAVEL, LLC**
201 Swanton Way
Decatur, Georgia 30030-3271
SAN: 254-6558
All orders will be shipped immediately on receipt.

RETAIL SHIPPING INFORMATION
Shipping and Handling in the U.S.

Retail price $29.95 per copy. Please include $4.00 for the first book. $1.00 for each additional book. For Priority Mail: Enclose $6.00 for the first book, $2 for each additional book. For additional information about international delivery or for multiple copy order discounts please contact us at: **info@europeincontext.com**

Name _____

Address _____

City _____ State _____ Zip_____

Telephone _____

Email address _____

Georgia residents add 5% sales tax; Ohio residents add 6.25% sales tax

Payment   Check   Credit card:

Visa, Mastercard, Discover, AMEX, Optima

Card number _____

Name on card _____

Exp. Date _____/_____ (mm/yy)

Venice In Context
The Independent Traveler's Guide to Venice
is distributed to the book trade by:
Independent Publishers Group
814 North Franklin St.
Chicago, IL 60610
Phone: (312) 337-0747
Orders Only (800)888-4741
Orders: orders@ipgbook.com
Customer Service: frontdesk@ipgbook.com